Distributor Survival
in the 21st Century

Distributor Survival in the 21st Century

Gordon Graham

INVENTORY MANAGEMENT PRESS
Richardson, Texas

Art Credits

Distributor Magazine, published by Technical Reporting Corporation, Chicago, Illinois.

Construction Equipment Distribution Magazine, published by the Associated Equipment Distributors, Oak Brook, Illinois.

The Welding Distributor Magazine, published by Penton Publishing, Cleveland, Ohio.

Electrical Wholesaling Magazine, published by Intertec Publishing Corporation, New York, NY.

Mr. Jack Schmidt, 3805 Candlelight Drive, Camp Hill, PA 17011.

This book was designed and typeset by Publications
Development Company, Crockett, Texas
Designer: James W. Land
Production Manager: Jean Brasher

For more information or additional copies contact

Inventory Management Press
P.O. Box 832795
Richardson, Texas 75083-2795

Library of Congress Cataloging in Publication Data available.

Printing *(last digit):* 9 8 7 6 5 4 3 2 1

Printed in the United States of America

DEDICATION

To my Lord and Savior, Jesus Christ
Who is both a light to the Gentiles and
for the Jews,
the Messiah,
the long-awaited "Anointed One."

Contents

Introduction

Why **another** book about distributors, the future, computers and inventory control? It's a good question . . . right? Some of you have labored through two books over the years written by Gordon Graham. "Certainly he's told us everything he knows!" you say. Well, if indeed you did read "Automated Inventory Management For the Distributor (1980) and "Distribution Inventory Management For the 1990's" (1987), you've absorbed a lot of "Grahamology" . . . but not quite all. Wholesale Distribution is a very dynamic industry. It changes all the time. New ideas keep popping up. Central warehousing, systems contracting, bar coding, EDI, fourth-generation computer languages, caller-identification, growth of huge distributors by acquisition, a renewed emphasis on the "Quality" process . . . all these and more keep affecting (and altering) the way you should operate as you move on through the 1990's and into the 21st century.

Distributors Come in Many Colors

The distribution business is fragmented also. A plumbing/heating/cooling distributor is another critter entirely from the guy in furniture or medical supplies. This peculiarity frustrates the computer software developers. For years, they've tried to offer one basic package to all three distributors. They can't, of course . . . not if they expect the system to do a good job, because this fragmentation is even more pronounced than in manufacturing, or retailing, or the "Physical Distribution" industry (the manufacturers moving their products out to the market through their own warehouses). So . . . ol' Graham feels honor-bound to emphasize a bunch of stuff you'd better consider as you look at the software offered to you . . . if you're in wholesale distribution.

Graham Concepts Require Some Groundrules and Disciplines

This third book is needed also for the rather large group of distributors who've followed my ideas, formulas, and procedures (and, remarkably, are still in business). Although I definitely favor the "KISS" approach in mathematics and control calculations, there are prerequisites to success in several areas. Certainly there are also exceptions where the basic formulas must be adjusted or set aside entirely. "Why didn't you tell us all this stuff the first time?" you ask. Any attempt at such a complete treatment in one volume would have resulted in something that looked like (and weighed the same as) an encyclopedia. Nobody would have read it at all. This book . . . hopefully my last . . . will cover these exceptions, modifications, and groundwork. Maybe *now* I can go live in Kauai or somewhere.

Picking a Software Package Is Still Dangerous

Although by now this shouldn't be true, distributors still must be very careful in selecting their next software package. There are *still* bad ones out there in the market who lure uninformed wholesalers into spending a big wad of cash for a "Me, Too" system. So this book expands the areas for you to check carefully, software features to demand (or to avoid), and offers predictions about the future . . . the role of the systems house as they affect you, the new emphasis on training, and new roles for some of the people in your company.

New Ideas Appear Continually

Even at my advanced age, a good portion of the work I do involves consulting with distributors and with software firms. These assignments often help me as much as I help them. As I study and critique what they're doing, I run onto a new way of solving a difficult problem . . . something nearly every distributor battles. Perhaps the software has a truly outstanding new feature which enhances user-productivity or makes one of my procedures more-easily learned and used. You need to hear about these improvements, and this book offers a way to get the ideas into your company and/or your system. Yes . . . I run some risk of "giving away" other peoples' secrets, but with any important breakthrough, the developer must realize that the idea won't be his private domain for long . . . no matter how careful his protective measures. If it really helps distributors run their businesses better, he should *want* others to hear about it.

LET'S GET UNDERWAY

Understand before you begin that this book is unlike my first two. Those offered a "system" of managing inventories: How to figure usage, lead times, ordering controls, when and how much to buy, etc. I'm not going back here to rehash all that stuff in depth. To understand much of what I'll say in this book, you should have first read "Distribution Inventory Management For The 1990's." This is a "companion" or followup book to that one. You'll be in the dark in several chapters here if you're unfamiliar with the earlier material. You'll also find these topics to be wider in scope: Enhancements to the earlier ideas; modifications; completely new subjects not covered at all in the earlier books; pitfalls to avoid in implementing the Graham concepts; and some general "fleshing out" in several areas.

It's a kind of potpourri . . . a mixture . . . of many topics, ideas, warnings, and refinements. The subjects move one to another on occasion without much transition, and you may get a bit confused . . . unless you're wide awake. The material can serve as a reference, however, to specific problems you may have run into as you tried to put my control concepts in place in your company or your software system. The book serves a valid purpose. Get a fresh cup of coffee, and let's get underway.

Distributor Survival
in the 21st Century

How A Distributor Will Survive in the 21st Century

1

Wow . . . the 21st Century!! Sounds like something out of Star Trek or 2001 or some other science fiction movie. The 1900's changing into the 2000's. The mere thought of moving into another century . . . another millennium yet . . . makes us all a bit nervous. What waits out there? What changes are in store for us and our children? Will there be war, peace, growth, higher taxes, inflation or recession? Will our economies in North America (U.S. and Canada) withstand the escalating national debts? Will distributors still be needed? If so, how will they function to be competitive? How will they survive?

The Hazy Future of Distribution

No one has reliable answers to such questions about the future, of course, although most of us can guess pretty accurately on taxes, the national debt, and inflation. The role of distributors is much more hazy. The growth of giant distributors in certain industries, the resurgence of buying groups, the tendency of big distribution customers to restrict their number of sources, the exact role of technology, the need to sell a distributors' value rather than only the products' prices . . . all these are going to have significant impact. The distributor's survival in such a swirl of movement and change will depend, I believe, on how quickly he adopts some new attitudes about his business.

View the Inventory as Dollar Bills

The first mandatory attitude adjustment will be the removal of the distributor's "rose-colored glasses" through which he previously saw inventory items when he walked out into the warehouse. In the future, he will simply see dollar bills in another form. The boss doesn't see cutting tools, or pipe, or fittings, fasteners, air compressors, coils of copper tubing, stacks of paper, reels of wire or hose, or whatever product is his specialty. He sees ones, fives, twenties and hundreds . . . greenbacks . . . all neatly stacked there on the shelves. Oh sure, the stuff really is in another form, but the president can't afford to view it that way. He or she *MUST* see its value only.

Think about that for a minute. If today you somehow magically transformed in your mind your current inventory into the dollars represented, how would you treat the stuff? Would you permit it to be handled (or mishandled) as it is now? Would you let the dollar bills gather dust? On December 31st, would you place still another inventory sticker on that big group of hundreds over in the corner? Would you let people make substitutes (three fives for a ten) but say nothing to the record-keepers about it? Would samples leave the building without paperwork? Would your "vault" be an open house, with everyone in the company, the neighborhood, and the county wandering in and out as they pleased . . . some filling their own orders, others using a little for repair work, and a few just helping themselves for personal needs? Would you let a salesman cause you to put $5000 out there on a whim . . . hoping he'll move the stuff out at a profit, but with no commitment to do so from him or anyone else?

Hmmm . . . of course not. Most if not all of these practices would stop pronto, or certainly some pretty careful procedures would be put in place if you were in fact dealing with negotiable currency . . . the "long green with a short future" . . . instead of water heaters, grinding wheels, bearings, or pumps. The point is clear: The inventory for a distributor is likely his largest asset. It must be ordered, received, put away, moved, customer orders filled, counted, protected, and records kept in a manner worthy of its value and status. Today, in many distributors' operations, it isn't. That must change if you intend to survive after 2000. You must see dollar bills on your shelves and develop (perhaps all-new) procedures to treat the inventory accordingly.

RECORD ACCURACY

For example, how many stock items in your warehouse at this moment have a precisely correct balance shown in your computer? 80 out of 100? 60 of 100? 25 of 100? If, instead, those were accounts in your bank, wouldn't it be comforting to learn that the accuracy rate was 60 accounts out of 100? You'd sorta hope that your account was one of the 60 . . . and you'd get your money out of that place as soon as possible (or when the FDIC paid off).

Why don't you check your item accuracy rate? For most distributors today, if it's been any length of time since your last annual physical inventory, you're down around 70% accurate. 30% of the stock items have incorrect balances shown in the computer. The 70% are mostly slow-movers . . . dusty stuff that nobody wants to steal. The 30% are the fast-moving popular products, so it's not much of a problem . . . right? WRONG! It's a disaster. What difference does it make that you've employed proven inventory control formulas for when & how much to order or just SWAG (Scientific, Wild-Ass Guesswork) . . . if you don't know what's out in the warehouse on an item? The benefits of the great formula will never be your's.

A "Day's-Work-In-A-Day" discipline becomes essential as the foundation on which to develop a program of Cycle Counting . . . which in turn generates very accurate stock balances. We'll discuss Cycle Counting again in Chapter 7, as well as the Day's-Work-In-A-Day environment necessary to make it work. I'll show you a software enhancement to make the entire Cycle Count process much more workable, but here we're talking about new attitudes the distributor should adopt. D-W-I-A-D certainly heads the list. Just as the bank maintains a "caught-up" mode daily on paperwork and currency location in the facility, the distributor must also . . . every night, every transaction, every item, every shelf, every branch. Tougher than the bank's problem? Yes. It doesn't matter. It still has to happen.

Productivity and Quality

One of the hot topics as I write this book is the "Quality Process" distributors are adopting. Frankly, it isn't all that new in concept (except to distributors). It boils down to this: "It's tougher, more time-consuming, more costly, and irritates customers more when you screw up and have to do something over . . . than if you'd done it right the first time." Redundant steps need to be removed throughout the company's operation. Sloppy, careless employees need first to be better trained and motivated . . . and then eliminated if they won't change. Departments should cooperate with and assist each other, rather than degenerating into an "Us/ Them" contest.

Brilliant? Revolutionary? Of course not. It's common sense, but for many reasons distributors are just now recognizing the importance of running a business this way. In the future, however, survival will depend on running lean (with inventory), efficient, with every employee very productive. Quality won't be some new program requiring "teams" to implement. It'll be a way of life. Top management, middle management, branch managers, sales personnel, purchasing employees, warehousemen, data processing, accounting . . . everybody will be on the "team" automatically. If you work here, you'll work productively. You'll work smart. You won't be careless or sloppy . . . or you simply won't work here!

The Computer System Must Promote This . . .
Not Drag It Down

There's no question today that the computer plays a massive role in what a distributor does. The manual-system joins mechanical calculators, slide rules, 78 RPM records, 8-track tapes, and one-platoon football as "systems" that served well in their time but are obsolete now. The computer has taken over . . . to say the least. What's a

bit frightening is *how much* impact the machine will have in the future. Everything will be touched by the computer. It'll help each step or procedure . . . expanding on the human operator's ability to perform . . . or it'll retard or inhibit what he or she can do. Frankly, the computer will assume one of two roles in your company: It'll be "Superman" fighting the forces of evil (bankruptcy or profit loss) . . . or it'll be a "Frankenstein Monster" running amuk in some operations with no way to control the thing.

We'll talk more in the next chapter about ways to be sure you pick a good system rather than one in the "monster" category. I'll expand on some of the warnings and exhortations from my 1987 book. Here, the emphasis is simply that the computer *IS* part of the Quality Process. You'll have a tough time implementing a quality operation if your "monster" system keeps inhibiting and slowing everyone down. If they must leave their desks, for example, to find information the computer should have provided or to perform a step it should have done for them . . . lousy productivity. Poor quality. That's the point.

AN EXAMPLE OF COMPUTER-ENHANCED PRODUCTIVITY

Any grand pronouncement like I've just made is nice to hear, but I must show you precisely what I mean. Let's take some time to delve into the type of computer-assisted productivity you must develop or buy in the future. My example is the new capability named "Caller-Identification." . . . the ability of the telephone system to identify an incoming caller, and then hookup with the computer to help the distributor avoid some time-wasting steps or missteps. It's now possible to tie your telephone system into your computer such that an incoming caller is identified as you pick up the receiver. Imagine saying to the customer (instead of "ABC Supply. Jack speaking"):

"Hi, Teri. Happy birthday!"

The customer thinks you're psychic. You're not. The telephone system identified the digits of the calling telephone. It then went to the computer files to see if that number was recorded. It found it for Ajax Industries and noted that Ms. Teri Lewis is the buyer who always calls you with orders, to check prices, or to expedite an old order. The file also had Teri's birthday . . . which happens to be today. All that information was flashed to your inside telephone salesman's screen as he picked up the call.

No More "Alpha-Search" Required

Obviously, Teri's birthday is a pretty silly use of this capability . . . but think of the other things you'd like to know about Teri's company before anything further is said:

1. Ajax Industries is now over their approved credit limit.
2. They have six delivery locations.
3. They won't pay invoices unless their purchase order number or the job number appears on them.
4. Ajax doesn't accept substitutes.
5. They don't like backorders. "Shorts" are to be cancelled.
6. Ajax has numerous items with specially-quoted prices.
7. Teri is an avid Chicago Bears fan; has three children named Mark, Chris, and Karen; and went to Notre Dame.

All this information appears on a special "critical data" screen for your inside telephone salesman . . . *BEFORE* a word is said by the customer! The customer is identified by (and for) the computer. The salesman need no longer key some part of the customer's name so that the computer can search its files to present all customers on the screen with similar names . . . to allow the salesman to select the right one. If that incoming phone number is in the computer file, you **KNOW** who's on the other end of the line!

The Advantages? Tremendous!

No matter what this customer intends to do, you no longer have to identify her for the computer. If ol' Teri wants to place a new order, the salesman hits a couple of keys and the order entry screen appears with Ajax Industries information already shown in the heading. If Teri wants instead to check a price, the salesman just keys the item number . . . and Teri's special price appears. This could be very important if the customer is playing games . . . doesn't tell you who it is . . . and asks a price. Or calls two of your branches to see which will quote the lower price . . . or if the caller is a competitor who asks your price but doesn't identify himself.

Expediting an Old Order

Maybe the customer just wants you to check an old order. When can she expect delivery? The salesman keys the item number. The computer searches for the first open sales order for Ajax Industries with that item on it, determines the purchase order it'll be coming in on, and displays the date that P.O. is due. Teri has her answer in five seconds.

The Credit Problem

If Ajax is over its credit limit . . . or a new order would put them there . . . the salesman can deal with the problem before the customer hangs up. "Listen Teri, I'll have to transfer you up to Louise in our Credit Department before I can promise delivery of this new order." . . . or, "Teri, your driver will have to bring a check when he comes over to pick this up today."

Don't let the customer hang up thinking everything's OK. If you do . . . and then you have to call her back tomorrow morning to say you can't ship the order, you can imagine her response: "Why didn't you tell me all this yesterday afternoon when I called in the order? I could have done something about it right then! Now you've really fouled me up. I need this stuff!" Poor quality . . . in how you handled a problem that should have been identified very early on for your salesman by the computer.

Not Every Salesman Enters the Order

You may be thinking: "Shoot. That's no big deal. Our Order Entry system tells us when a customer is over the credit limit" . . . or "It tells us if a customer has special prices when the order is keyed in." True . . . most systems today do exactly that. Trouble is, our salesman isn't going to enter the order. He's going to scribble it down on a phone order pad and hand the order to Agnes, who keys all our new orders. By that time, of course, the customer is long gone off the phone. Agnes will get all the benefits of our great interactive order entry system . . . but she'll have to bring back to the salesman any problems the computer identifies, and the salesman will have to call the customer back. Lost motion. Telephone tag, etc.

This special "Critical Data" screen alerts the salesman to vital facts he should know or be sure to ask before the customer leaves the phone. If there are several delivery addresses, ask which one this order goes to. The customer's employee may be new . . . doesn't know to tell you, or assumes that you know. If he doesn't give you the job number, ask for it. Don't let him leave the phone without telling you. If you do, your company may be 120 days collecting the invoice . . . countless manhours will have to be expended by your employees to get your money. Sorry productivity, and your profits suffer.

Saving an Order

Let's say that the customer begins giving your salesman a new order, which he's writing down on an order form for entry later by

Agnes. Knowing that the customer won't accept substitutes might lead your salesman to say: "Teri, I know you don't usually take subs, but all I can provide on this third item is Brand B. We've been out of the brand you want for quite a while. Could I send Brand B this one time?" The customer may say no . . . .but once in a while the response might be: "Well OK this one time. Just don't make a practice of it!" You've saved the order. Had Agnes just keyed in the order with Brand A, the computer would have cancelled the item.

That's why I care (in Inventory Management) about such computer breakthroughs. We bought the inventory to SELL! I want every advantage the computer can offer to help me do that . . . not lose an order, price something wrong, reject an order for credit, or ship it to the wrong place . . . because the computer system didn't provide a way for the right person to check these things at the proper time. This new technology fills a gap in most of the current computer systems. It enhances productivity . . . yes, but it also gets the stock sold.

The Concept Isn't All That New

This "Caller ID" capability is becoming ever more common. It's now used by the Emergency agencies in your city. When a child calls the 911 number to say that "Mommy is sick!" . . . the operator sees on a screen the address of the calling number. In many states today, the telephone companies are offering this feature on a small dial for your home phone. Just think of the benefits to a distributor when that same capability is harnessed.

An Example of a Problem Eliminated

One distributor I know has a single customer with 70 delivery addresses. When one of these locations called with an order, the telephone salesmen didn't want to admit that they couldn't recognize the caller's voice and have to ask who it was. Often they'd guess . . . and then the material would be shipped to the wrong place. Not any longer. Every caller is clearly identified. No more misdirected shipments.

Is This an Invasion of Privacy?

In this era of super-sensitivity about getting sued by nearly anyone over any tiny real or imagined slip-up, this telephone/computer capability might be construed as invading the privacy of the caller. I'd take the risk. My question to the caller: "Why did you call us if you don't want us to know who you are? What kind of illegal or unethical game are *you* playing?" If the caller wants to remain anonymous, there are always pay phones where the numbers wouldn't be recorded in my computer.

Certain groups are lobbying Congress, however, to make this whole process illegal. They *don't want* that dial on your home telephone telling you the calling number if the phone rings while you're having dinner. The dial may one day say that it's XYZ Carpet Cleaning Service on the line. XYZ claims that it's an invasion of their privacy for you to know who's calling and perhaps not answer. How about **MY** privacy, buster?

Yes, there are a few legitimate problems. If you call some business just for information, they'll have your number recorded and might then start mailing you stuff or call back to try to make sales. However, this technology benefits businesses tremendously who take many orders by telephone. It has far more advantages than disadvantages. All the legal hassles will be worked out. At worst, you might have to get a signed release from the important customers allowing you to identify them when they call. Most should want you to do it. It speeds up your handling of their order or inquiry. It increases their productivity in buying from you.

Get In Touch With Your Telephone System

My counsel: Call the company from whom you bought or lease your telephone system. Ask them if they can offer this capability in your area. Then, call your computer software outfit or your programmer. Have them do some research on this and be ready to start programming the computer tie-in as soon as the telephone equipment can do its part. You may be surprised to learn that your telephone system has been able to identify incoming digits from Day 1 of your installation, . . . but didn't bother to mention this to you because they saw no application in your business.

Prophecy: This Capability Will Soon Be Commonplace

You don't want to be the last kid on your block with such a computer/telephone tie-in. Think of all the benefits:

- Added productivity of telephone personnel;
- Reduced risk of critical information going unscreened when a customer's order is taken;

- The impression left with a customer when you provide in seconds a vast array of facts he might want, accurately, without asking him who he is;
- Never having to tell the computer (on any additional screens) who the customer is, once you pick up the phone;
- The reduced manhours needed today in your business to clean up problems created by not getting the customers' facts straight (or guesswork) at any point in your initial conversation with him.

This feature is so valuable, so important to distributors that every telephone system and computer will have this capability soon. You'd better be sure that you do early on.

PRODUCTIVITY WILL MAKE THE DIFFERENCE FOR MANY DISTRIBUTORS

Most distributors are mid-sized. They have sales of between $5 million and $20 million per year . . . but they must compete in some cases and locations with really huge outfits. One of the trends we're seeing today is the emergence of great, huge distributors who continue to buy smaller companies and move in ever-widening circles, geographic areas, and markets. Shoot, there's nothing wrong with that. More power to 'em . . . if they can pull it off and stay healthy. That's just the "good ol' American Way." It does, however, change . . . or *should change* . . . the mid-sized distributor's philosophy about how to avoid being gobbled-up yourself.

How in the world can you expect to compete with the giant's buying power and ability to sell at lower prices in your market? How can you sell at his prices and stay alive? The answer . . . Productivity! The giant is like an elephant crashing through the jungle. If you're a rabbit, stay out of his path. He'll crush you if you meet him head-on. On the other hand, Mr. Rabbit, you can run circles around him. You're much more elusive, much more able to move in any direction quickly than the ponderous elephant. You're much quicker on your feet . . . much more responsive.

You can compete with him through enhanced productivity . . . supported in turn by a computer system that's better than his. Your people aren't as numerous. They're better paid (We'll talk about that in Chapter 8). They're better trained. You keep them longer. They do more work, quicker and more efficiently, than do the big boy's people. Your cost-per-sales-dollar is lower than his. You can sell at his low prices (when you have to) and make as much net as he does through his buying power with the suppliers.

Think about the giant distributors you know. They have a continual problem getting and keeping good people. They wrestle with "size" headaches. Decisions take longer to make. Great hosts must be indoctrinated, convinced, and trained before new procedures take effect. It's hard to police what employees do out in the far-flung network. Effecting a major course-correction is like the elephant . . . ponderous and time-consuming.

Compare This to How the Smaller Distributor Moves

Now think about the better distributors you know who are small or mid-sized. Decisions don't require a huge committee's study, recommendation and approval. Things happen quickly. The boss decides . . . people act. Programs are introduced in days instead of months. Of necessity, employees must perform more than one task, but that develops more-knowledgeable, more-experienced people who can get things done. They know who to call; they don't have to ask. They know who performs a needed service in town; they don't have to call around to find out. They know more about more products. The big distributor develops "specialists" to a degree. The smaller guy has "general practitioners."

An Example from Football

A pro football team offers an example of what I'm driving at here. They have a specialist to kick off or punt. If the returner gets by those other specialists out there, the kicker's usually in trouble. He's supposed to stop the return man, but he really isn't trained to do that very well. If he does make the tackle, everyone's amazed. Now on a small college team, that kickoff man is likely a regular player who just happens to also do the kicking. He's much better trained and able to make a tackle if he has to. He's a more productive player . . . overall . . . because he has more than one skill. Maybe it's a poor analogy, but that's how I see the smaller distributor holding his own in the 21st century with the giants. He'll get more from each player. His people will become more skilled in the use of their computer, and very likely the system itself will be better.

The Smaller Company Has an Edge in Computer Software

A very large, multi-branch distributor usually develops his own software because he can't find anything on the market to handle his wide-ranging requirements. Often, the system he winds up with lacks one or more important functions, restraints, or performs calculations in his time-honored ways. It must accommodate long-standing practices that are definitely non-productive but are ". . . the way we've always done it." The smaller distributor on the other hand has access today to some *very good* software packages that are fairly quickly installed. His requirements aren't so complex or set in stone by years of habit. He moves much more quickly (like the rabbit) into the better, no-big-voids system and reaps the benefits long before his giant competitor reaches the same point. He changes his operating philosophy right along with the mechanics of the new software.

That's how you'll survive, Mr. or Ms. mid-sized distributor, as you move on out of the 1990's and into the 21st century. Productivity . . . quality in the people and operation . . . accuracy . . . excellent use of resources . . . no lost motion . . . inventory viewed and handled as dollars . . . productivity-enhancing computerized system . . . quick in your response to needed changes . . . that's how you'll make it.

The New Role of Computers in the Future

2

As the last chapter said, a distributor's computer in the 21st century will assume the role of Superman or a Frankenstein Monster. It'll be the most valuable tool your company has to help you improve people productivity, operate with low inventories, and cut down on lost motion . . . or it'll be a big "millstone," dragging down all efforts to keep your head above the competitive waters. In short, it'll make or break you.

Stay Off the Freeway in Your Horse & Buggy

A good analogy is the automobile. Look how it changed everyone's life and offered all kinds of new opportunities, once it became a regular part of every household. A person could live in one part of town but work in another as far as 20-30 miles away. The family could take trips that were out of the question with ol' Dobbin and the buggy. The time required for travel was reduced greatly, and after a few more developments, a trip changed from an ordeal to a much more pleasant experience . . . but what happened to those people who said: "You'll never see *ME* ridin' in one of those new-fangled contraptions!"? Or the guy who preferred his Model T when other people now had 8-cylinder, automatic transmission, air-conditioned, steel-belted-tire models? Talk about poor productivity . . . or the ability to compete in a race . . . boy, that poor devil was left in everyone's dust (literally).

That's how I see the better computerized systems of the future, compared to some of the stuff on the market today. That new system you'll select sometime in the 1990's to take you into the 21st century has the potential of giving you a Lexus vs. Model T advantage . . . an advantage you're going to need to compete against the super-competitor discussed in the last chapter who can eat you alive with his buying power.

HOW TO GO WRONG PICKING A SYSTEM

Since your next system will be so critical, let's discuss a few of the pitfalls you must avoid in the selection or development process. If you read my 1987 book, you'll recall that I mentioned some of these:

1. Falling victim to the "Field/Tent" Syndrome
2. Picking hardware first . . . then looking for software

There are more.

Open Versus Proprietary Operating Systems

Some years back, if you went shopping for a VCR (video recorder), you had to make a decision between Beta models or VHS. At that early stage, the verdict was still out as to which type would dominate. There were advantages in both systems. Today if you buy Beta, you'll have serious trouble finding very many tapes that will play. The verdict's no longer in doubt. VHS has won. I'm sure there are still video purists who argue: "Beta is superior!" Maybe it is, maybe not . . . it doesn't really matter any more.

That's the way it is right now with a computer requiring a "proprietary" operating system, compared to a machine using an "open" system. Yes, I *know* there are long-winded arguments still raging about the merits of one system over the other . . . but like Beta/VHS, it really doesn't matter. The open system is definitely winning. Operating systems of one of the Unix varieties, or perhaps

Pick, run on many different computers. The proprietary systems run on just one brand.

Hardware Improvements

Recent years have seen a virtual explosion of computers with capabilities unheard of just a short time ago. I know only enough about hardware to be dangerous, but even to my unskilled eye it's amazing what these critters will do for the money . . . compared to the old days. The processing speeds and ability to support large numbers of terminals and printers keep improving at a rate that boggles my mind. Another amazing fact: The doggone things are a lot more reliable than they used to be. A host of manufacturers (some unknown a few years back) produce truly excellent machines that rarely break down. And the costs . . . heck, they just keep on coming down relative to what the machines can do.

You Don't Want to Get Locked-In to Any Particular Brand

So the first pitfall to avoid is selecting software that runs only on one supplier's specific line of computers. You're locked-in if you do. You can't change. You can't move to some other guy's fantastic equipment with a 21st century breakthrough . . . and still run your same basic programs. You must wait for your supplier to catch up. You should select software in the "Open Systems" mode, designed to run on several "platforms" (computer brands or types). Avoid anyone's "proprietary" equipment or operating system. If the software you're considering runs on only one box . . . forget it. You don't want a Model T.

PROGRAMMING LANGUAGES

Here we go again. Are forth-generation languages superior to third-generation systems? What's the advantage of one over the other? Can't a 3rd-GL do the same things a 4th-GL can? Does Gordon Graham really know? I can sure answer that last one: "No, he doesn't!" The experts tell me, however, that programming is much easier in a fourth-generation language. 100 lines of code

cause the computer to execute the same steps that would have required 1000 lines in a third-generation language. Programming
changes are easier, modular systems are easier to develop, and the
machine itself works more efficiently.

By the time you read this book, there may be fifth-generation
languages, and I guess the 21st century will see some in the 10th-
GL category at some point. My counsel today is to select the fourth-
generation version over the 3rd-GL if the basic features and other
benefits appear equal. Remember . . . productivity is always an
issue. If you have your own programmers, or you're paying some
outside firm to program for you, you always want them to get the
job done with a minimum of effort and use as little time as possible.
You don't want old-fashioned software where every modification
request required you to float a loan, and you were too old to use the
new feature when it was finally ready.

Machine Efficiency

I really don't understand how computers work. I'm not sure I want
to. I can barely program my VCR. An answering machine likewise
presents all the programming challenges I can handle. It stands to
reason, however, that if 100 lines of code makes my computer get a
job done . . . the machine works less than if 1000 lines of code
had to be read and processed for the same step. And even though
the computers of the future will be more powerful and may cost
less per "mip" (or whatever) than today, they sure won't be inexpensive. The distributor wants his equipment to function at maximum efficiency. It appears to a layman like me that a 4th-GL
language-system just has to cause a computer to perform better.
You won't need that additional memory as soon as you would with
a less-efficient language telling the critter what to do.

"CLIENT-SERVER" OR THE WORKSTATION CONCEPT

Even though I understand only basic computer operating principles,
certain concepts make sense. One of these is the new "Client-
Server" . . . sometimes called "Workstation" . . . method of
configuring your system. The idea is to offload much of what your

main CPU (Central Processing Unit) does onto individual personal computers scattered around the company. If you have several remote branches, some very real benefits accrue. The main computer back in the home office uses its tremendous power more in a data management mode than in acting as a "traffic cop" over the various window applications for terminals in the branches . . . and the expanding use of windows is becoming ever more important in every system. The windows are managed instead by the individual PC's.

Take It A Step Further: Add Some Duplicate Files in the Branches

If you go one step further and put copies of certain relatively static files on the PC's, the branch system becomes much more autonomous. Much of the information you need in Order Entry, for example, resides in the branch's own computer. Things like customer files, supplier files, pricing, static stock item information . . . are all in the local system. The home office computer provides only the highly-variable information, like quantity available for sale, etc. The advantages:

1. If the main computer goes down, the branch still continues to operate. Yes, some information isn't available to it, but orders can still be taken, printed, and moved out the door. You are *not* shut down.

2. The amount of data that must be transmitted between the main computer and the branch system is reduced by as much as 50% or more. Order Entry goes much smoother, much more quickly. The system is more efficient.

3. The computer back in the home office can be smaller. You don't need the huge processing "hog" that's required when all you have in the branches are terminals that have no internal files of their own.

Graham, You're Contradicting What You Said in an Earlier Book

OK, I know I'm saying something different here than in my 1987 book. There I made an issue of *NOT* duplicating file information.

Static or relatively static information was to be in just one file . . . with all others drawing what they needed as required. What's happened to change my mind? Personal computers are getting so good, so fast, and capable of storing so much information considering the cost . . . that the old rules aren't nearly as important as in the 80's. The use of windows has also become very widespread, but "managing" the windows takes an awful lot of computer firepower. When the home office system has to do that for ten branches, the computer has to be a lot bigger if it's also to do all its other processing and not slow everyone down too much.

The Costs May Even Be a Trade-off

By the time you read this, the cost of mainframes and PC's will likely be down even more than as I write. You likely can buy a smaller mainframe, put PC's of the $1200–1500 variety in each branch, and come out less than today's more common structure of a big home office computer and only terminals in the branches. My suggestion: Look for a system structured to function in this manner. Make sure the software you're considering supports this mode.

LOOSEY-GOOSEY SYSTEMS

Another pitfall to step around is the "loosey-goosey" software package. Let's define that: A loosey-goosey system allows so much flexibility in how a buyer operates that he or she can do almost anything they want to in any ordering situation. The system allows almost unlimited versatility in how the captured usage or lead time data is worked into the ordering controls. In fact, the ordering controls can be anything the buyers want. There are no restraints. There are no guidelines programmed into the system . . . other than those inserted (or programming requested) by the buyers. Any stock item in any branch location may be handled under a myriad of methods . . . and the buyer or branch manager simply decides which to use, where and when.

What's Wrong with That?

On the surface, such software appears OK. In fact, it's sold with this tremendous versatility and flexibility as a major strongpoint. "You can control an item any way you want to with our package!" . . . brags the salesman. So why do I counsel you away from this system?

Asset management . . . or rather mismanagement . . . is the Number 1 cause of distributor failure today. Distributors carry far more inventory than they need. They buy badly. They buy too much of the wrong things and not enough of others. They strive to get the lowest-possible cost on an item from a supplier to enable their salesmen to be competitive . . . but in the process, ignore all other economic factors. Branch managers tend to keep far more stock than is really needed to be sure they can service the customers.

How do they get by with all this? How do these conditions evolve? The people making the buying decisions do so *by their own rules*. They use their own SWAG. Each follows a different drummer, so to speak, but always with one overriding objective: "Take care of the customers. Don't **ever** run out of stock!" The computer system makes no real attempt to modify what the buyers do. It certainly doesn't restrain them. It simply gives them the information. Each person uses the data however they wish. SWAG rules, assisted by the computer. The company ignores the fact that lack of sales is ranked *Number 7* as a cause of bankruptcy in distribution today. Mismanaged assets . . . too much inventory, moving too slowly . . . is Number 1.

How Will This Change in the Future?

Effective asset-management software in the future (and even some today) takes another attitude entirely. Such unlimited flexibility in the hands of a "sales-dominated" buyer results in massive inventories. He or she must be guided. He must be restrained. You young mothers would never say to your six-year-old child:

> "Honey, here's a BB pistol, a water gun and Daddy's loaded 45. I don't want you to be restrained. Play with whichever toy you want to while I'm out shopping."

If the youngster selects the wrong "toy," he'll blow his head off. In today's economic climate, if a buyer uses the wrong ordering method under conditions that call for something else . . . he'll blow away your profits. The buyers need guidance and, at times, very definite restraint. Not only that, Top Management must act as a buffer. The Boss approves and supports the guidance/restraint principles. The President answers any salesman who criticizes the buyer's new groundrules.

The better software does indeed guide what a buyer's to do in given situations. It recommends when to buy, how much, lists the additional items to add to the order to make weight, and warns if a buyer decides to override and do it his way. Rules are programmed to restrain when stock can be "pirated" for customers in other branches (we'll re-visit this problem in Chapter 6).

Predictable Results . . . That's the Objective

Good software includes data capturing & use guidelines designed to produce predictable customer service and inventory turnover results. For example, I recommend six months' of history be used in forecasting usage, two lead times be averaged, a 50% safety allowance be employed as a minimum . . . and yes, I admit these are my own ground rules. I admit that they don't work for every stock item every time, and that exceptions must always be identified and handled independently. You'd have to read my 1987 book or view the 12-hour video course to get all the details about this.

The point here: These groundrules . . . this "system" produces predictable results. Service is excellent. Turnover is profitable . . . overall. The better software defaults to these guidelines and warns anyone who might start to make adjustments:

> "Hey, do you know what you're doing? Listen, you'd better be careful. You're violating a portion of an overall system designed to give good service and turns. Proceed with extreme caution, and by the way, you're on your own. If you don't have a very good reason for making this adjustment, the boss may be counseling you about your new career path."

At other times, the system tells a branch manager (in effect):

"Sorry. You can't have that material in Los Angeles that you want for your customer there in San Jose. The stock isn't there for your customer. It's in Los Angeles for L.A. area customers. You *can* have any L.A. surplus, but the regular inventory comes to you only with the approval of the L.A. manager."

An effective system all goes together to produce predictable results. Certainly, anyone might argue: "I prefer to do it another way." "I like to use 24 months of history," or only three with different weighting factors for each one. "We average the last six lead times." "I always keep 30 days of safety stock on every item." "We never order more than 60 day's stock on anything." "We'll take stock from any branch if we have a sale.". . . and on and on. "Furthermore, I want a software package that lets me do what I want in every facet!"

Hey, some of these ideas may be better than mine. That's not the point. They're only "pieces" in a total concept. Using an alternative somebody likes better on some control or method might yield superior results, but here's the problem: The results aren't predictable. The better software builds a complete system with interrelated data, controls, and procedures. The results *are* predictable.

Good Software Has Specific Restraints

Therefore, the really good software today is anything but loosey-goosey. It doesn't permit a buyer to do anything he pleases . . . at least, not without a warning. Restraints are in place to assure the highest percent possible of "Yes" answers to customers who want to order . . . rather than only one "Yes" followed by a string of "No's" in another branch. The restraints can't be overridden by anyone without proper authority. Be sure you find or develop a system that functions in a guided & restrained manner. Stay away from the loosey-goosey packages. You don't want one that lets your buyers keep doing all the bad things, use the same poor judgment they've used in the past . . . not if you want to bring your inventory down and improve customer service. Not if you'd like to be around as a business entity in the 21st century.

THE "INDUSTRY-VERTICAL" SYSTEM TRAP

This next phenomenon is by no means unique to distribution, but every distributor thinks that his business is different. The paper distributor sees no similarity between what he does and an electrical supply house. The industrial distributor (the old mill supply house) views a fluid power outfit as outside his realm. Certainly to a degree, they're right. Paper houses deal with fine & commercial paper plus sanitary supplies, and there are conversions required that the electrical guy avoids. Fluid power distributors have to make assemblies of components and often perform more design work on a sale than does the cutting tool salesman. Some industries are indeed worlds apart. The candy & tobacco distributor has little in common with a furniture wholesaler. Almost nothing they do or the problems they face are the same.

In Many Industries & Functions, They're Brothers

In the durable goods industries, however, the steps performed routinely from one distributor to another . . . especially in Inventory Management . . . are not much different. Arguments about the differences begin to evaporate like a morning fog when you really study what goes on. Oh sure, certain aspects of sales order entry, order processing, accounting, and sales reporting are unique to an industry. The Inventory Control requirements are *not* unique. Inventory items are stocked. They must be replenished. Decisions have to be made as to when and how many to bring in. Data must be captured to guide these decisions. The objectives are not to run out or have too much stock. Customers order in an independent mode most of the time.

Old Software Highlighted the Differences

One way a software house in the past attracted a distributor customer was to demonstrate clearly how well the unique aspects of his particular industry were handled in the package. "Bells & Whistles" were built in for conversions, pricing, order-handling, sales order entry, accounting, and sales reporting that truly solved some nasty headaches the distributor had battled for years. After a while, the software house could also produce a list of many other distributors in that same industry who had signed on. The combination of unique features and user list was overwhelming. The new guy never looked any further. He signed too.

Times Changed. The System Didn't

Now don't misunderstand: This approach was pretty smart. It worked. Several software firms grew rapidly through the 70's, 80's, and into the 90's by offering an "Industry Vertical" package. A few dominated a specific distributor market almost totally. In fact, they were so successful that they fell victim to the oldest business trap around: They rested on their laurels. Important elements of the package . . . like asset management . . . were not improved. Economic times changed, but the system didn't. Asset mismanagement became the Number 1 cause of distributor failure, but the package gave no real help to (or put no restraint on) the buyers. The glitzy features always sold the package in the past. Management figured they still would.

What's a Better Approach Today?

Today, there are software packages on the market that do a much better job with asset management. Buyers are helped, guided, restrained. Branch managers are likewise. Control calculations are simple, understandable, duplicatable by an average person with an average education in mathematics. Admittedly these packages don't have the bells & whistles your particular industry really needs in the other areas. In sales order entry features, for example, these asset-oriented systems might score only a 7 perhaps (on a scale of 1 to 10) against the more vertically-oriented package's sure-fire 10. That might be true in Accounting also.

However, the industry-specific package quite often scores only a 1 or maybe even a void in the critical asset-management, purchasing guidance/restraint, branch-transfer-control functions. Oh, they don't admit this of course. There's always some way to capture usage, guide the buying, etc. Reports come out that appear to prompt a buyer to take the necessary stock-replenishment steps . . . but often, any form of SWAG is encouraged and accepted. Any method of calculation may be used. There are no restraints to inhibit anything a salesman or manager wants to do. "Take care of the customer! Don't worry about the paperwork processing or what happens to inventory as a result! Hey, isn't this the way you built your business back in the 70's ?" . . . asks the systems salesman.

The Real Cost of Modifying the Two Systems

Either system approach you select requires modifications. If you purchase the asset control package, you must make modifications to bring each of its low-scoring features up to a 10. The cost for this? . . . maybe $ 20,000 in programming, and yes, you would have to spend this extra money. But if you opt for the vertical-industry package, you've often inherited several major "voids" in critical asset-management and/or restraint areas. It'll cost $250,000 in programming enhancements to fill in the voids or bring the 1's up to 10's. That's if you recognize the problem and know how to make the program changes to correct the shortcomings. Chances are, you won't notice the void until it bites you (bankruptcy). If you do sense a missing link somewhere, you may not have the expertise available to fix the software.

Go with a System That's Solid on All Fronts

You're better off, I believe, to take the less industry-specific package with no serious weaknesses in the asset-management areas . . . if it does a solid (although not absolutely superior for your industry) job in the other functions. Certainly, the original order entry steps must promote productivity. Yes, Accounting must be one of the best around. Order-handling can't be 1980's mode. Data must be captured to permit a very versatile query in every major category. Go ahead then and add the bells & whistles to this package. Spend the $ 20,000. Avoid the more-attractive system with the long list of users in your industry if it's too loosey-goosey or is just plain negligent in the asset-management functions.

BE ON GUARD AGAINST A COMMON SALES TECHNIQUE

If you were a salesman for one of the industry-specific or feature-specific packages . . . but knew it fell short in other areas . . . what would be your selling approach? Corner the person most affected by the problem(s) your system handles well. Show him or her what you have . . . then have some Valium ready to calm them down. They're going to get *very* excited about your system. If the system excels in Accounting, show it first to the Controller. Everybody knows that the Controller has a major voice in system-selection. If it has time and labor-saving features for Inside Sales, be sure the Sales Manager is present for your demo. With the Controller and Sales Manager on your side, shoot, the President is bound to go along with their recommendations.

Of course, be sure *NOT* to mention in any depth what the system does for Purchasing & Inventory Control . . . or if anyone does ask a question on some feature, you answer: "Oh sure, we handle that. No problem." There's a good chance they're so entranced with the super features they've seen already that they'll assume: "Boy, if these guys do all that other neat stuff so well, they really must know our business. They probably handle all other functions with equal skill." They won't press you for details.

You'd Better Know the Questions to Ask

An uneducated system-selector today is fair-game for this sales approach. Mr. President, *YOU* have to jump right in the fat middle of the system selection process. You must make sure that all functions are covered well by the new package . . . especially the asset-management steps. Be sure that the proper restraints are in place even if the Purchasing Manager sees them as invading on his or her domain. You must know enough to evaluate what your Controller says, judge the reasons behind the Sales Manager's enthusiasm for this system proposal, determine where your current asset management needs shoring-up, and be able to ask questions that pinpoint any weaknesses the proposed system may be hiding.

This Job Can't Be Delegated

Repeating a warning or two from the 1987 book, the new computerized system (in its effect on your company) will more closely resemble an airplane than a new heating unit. When your old heating unit finally quit and a new one was needed, you probably delegated the "system selection" process to the Operations Manager. Your task, as President, was to approve the expenditure. The approach worked just fine. The Operations Manager studied all the equipment on the market, picked one, and it turned out to be a truly energy-saving, low-maintenance unit.

Just don't try that with the next computer system. If the Controller is delegated the selection job, you may wind up with a system that keeps excellent records of how you went out of business. If it's wrong, you won't just be cold . . . you'll crash and burn. The computer acts more like an airplane in which the entire company will be flying along off the ground. The machine must serve every major business function very efficiently and productively. It must promote a quality operation throughout. It must encourage and maximize the benefits of a disciplined work environment. It must restrain when dangerous conditions are encountered. You've got trouble if it:

- Is underpowered and can't hold altitude in a snowstorm (recession)
- Is designed for long runways and your branches are grass strips
- Is not pressurized and competition forces you up to 40,000 feet
- Flames out when you apply full throttle trying to take off
- Tailspins when you make a tight turn (merger, acquisition, new market)
- Uses more fuel to go 300 miles than the tanks hold
- Requires expensive maintenance constantly to keep flying at all
- Lacks critical instruments to show that you're in a dive
- Has no warning buzzers or lights to indicate a stall
- Allows anyone to fly the thing from any seat
- Has no restraints like seat belts or control limiters

Sure, this is airplane talk . . . but there's a comparison in computer system functions. I see distributors all the time limping along with computers suffering from several distressing afflictions of this magnitude, but they sure get great meals from the fantastic galley. The seats swivel all the way around for good conversation, and the movie selection is second to none. Nice features . . . true, but not that expensive to add to a basically sound craft. On the other hand, fixing one of the problems in the list above would require a major airframe, instrumentation, engine, or wiring overhaul. Now perhaps you see my point about picking a system on glitzy features instead of knowing enough to evaluate overall performance . . . especially asset management.

LET'S MOVE ON

Picking a good system in the future is hazardous . . . no question about it, but fortunately there are more and more good ones becoming available. If you're too scared now to proceed in the search on your own, I'll repeat my offer from 1987 to send a list of the packages I consider the best. My address and telephone number appears later. Don't think about that right now. There's even more for you to consider first. There's more to learn, so you'll be in position to ask all the right questions of anyone offering a system. Read on so that you can truly be an educated system selector when the moment of critical truth arrives . . . and take a look at the illustration on page 30, so that (unlike me) you'll understand how computers really work.

COMPUTER CRASH COURSE

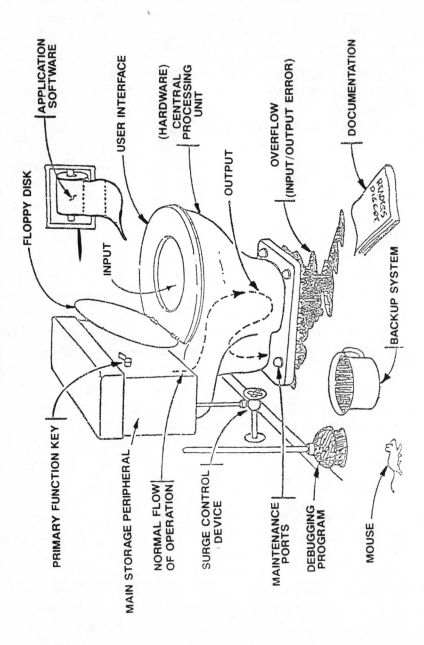

APPLICATION SOFTWARE

FLOPPY DISK

USER INTERFACE

INPUT

(HARDWARE) CENTRAL PROCESSING UNIT

OUTPUT

OVERFLOW (INPUT/OUTPUT ERROR)

DOCUMENTATION

PRIMARY FUNCTION KEY

MAIN STORAGE PERIPHERAL

NORMAL FLOW OF OPERATION

SURGE CONTROL DEVICE

MAINTENANCE PORTS

DEBUGGING PROGRAM

MOUSE

BACKUP SYSTEM

The New Role
of Training in
the Future

3

As distributors move through this last decade before the 21st century, it's natural to wonder what lies out there in our path. It's a popular topic these days. All kinds of predictions are being offered about products we'll be using . . . trends to expect . . . opportunities to seek out or problems to avoid . . . and forecasts of world conditions to anticipate. So it's appropriate also to consider how distributors will best be able to use their computers. What'll be necessary to get the maximum benefit from the truly outstanding new features the systems will contain?

Software Enhancements

As the 1990's move along, we're seeing dramatic improvements in the software . . . the computer programs . . . offered on the market to durable goods distributors. For years, distributors had to settle for "warmed-over" manufacturing systems . . . adaptations (sometimes "mutations") that really didn't address the unique Inventory Management and Purchasing headaches of the *wholesale* distributor.

A good example is "DRP" . . . Distribution Requirements Planning. DRP was born in the manufacturing industries as an off-shoot of "MRP" . . . Material Requirements Planning. It works pretty well for the manufacturer moving his products out to the market through his own warehouses . . . his own "controlled" distribution environment. This form of product movement is called "Physical Distribution." . . . but it's *not* "Wholesale Distribution." For most wholesale distributors, DRP works poorly if at all, unless very controlled conditions with a customer are present. Today, better and better systems are becoming available that are **not** mutations. They're designed for the pure wholesale-distribution industry by people who've taken the time to learn how "wholesalers" function, the problems they face, and have developed solid systems to help out.

What's Unique About the New Systems?

For one thing, these new packages demand a much higher skill level from a distributors' purchasing personnel than in years past. A buyer can no longer be ol' Jack who's too old to be out on the road selling any more, so another job's been found for him until retirement. It can't be "Agnes" either . . . who will work for $ 1200 a month, but really isn't too smart, won't work very hard, and would quit tomorrow if a better job turned up in town . . . or if you tried to put any pressure on her for improved performance.

The new systems require now . . . and ever so much more so in the future . . . a true purchasing "professional." The buyer must be well-paid; motivated to excel; trained to use new concepts, new controls, and skilled in using all the features the computer offers; and satisfied to remain in an area of the company other than Sales. These buyers spend millions today of the distribution company's money, and such numbers will get truly scary as you move past the year 2000. Developers of the new computerized systems recognize this and offer methods and capabilities to do the purchasing job very well.

Don't Turn Agnes Loose with a Tractor

Trouble is, for some distributors right now, such systems couldn't be turned over to their current buyers. It would be equivalent to letting some guy who'd used only a mule to plow a field step into the cab of a $50,000 tractor. Not only would the field be plowed. So would the highway, the farmhouse, and a sizable section of town. It's not a question of the system's efficiency compared to the old ways. It's an operator problem.

System Training Requirements in the Future

For this reason, the effective software of the future will require much more extensive (and expensive) "operator" training than in years past. Please . . . I'm referring to the Inventory Management . . . the Purchasing functions. *This* is where such new levels of training will be needed! This is the area that's lagged so far behind other company functions. Accounting in distribution has matured significantly. Warehousing functions, like bar coding, are coming of age. Sales-assistance is well-developed in most systems. But in the area of Inventory Management, most distributor software today is still much too "loosey-goosey." We talked about this in the last chapter. Almost anything a buyer wants to do . . . any buying concept at all . . . is permitted. The buyer isn't "nudged" to do the right thing for the conditions encountered.

Training Will Make Up a Major Portion of System Cost

This will change in the future. The effective computerized system will suggest specific steps, quantities, and actions in accord with the conditions to consider . . . and of course, the buyer must be trained to use the controls properly. This training will not be cheap. My prediction is that it won't be long before computer hardware costs X . . . the software costs 2X . . . and the training (properly administered) may be as much as 3X. Distributor executives must alter their thinking to accept this . . . or they'll have to settle for older-style systems that don't require such training, but of course are of the "mule" category. They'll have to compete with their mule against "tractors," and they won't like the results.

Watch Your Negotiating, Mr. President!

Most distributor executives are good negotiators. They've had to be to survive . . . and these negotiating skills are applied to every major expenditure. A computerized system's cost can be negoti-ated. You can haggle about many aspects of the overall package, especially with "Turnkey" systems where hardware, software, and training are all offered by one firm. My suggestion: Be careful! You might negotiate out some training costs that will be vital to the success of your system.

The Competitive Race of Your Future Requires a Jet

These better systems of the future will be as much improved over most current packages as an airplane is over a car. You can still drive from New York to California, of course, but a 747 gets there much faster and carries a whole lot more people. The distributor of the 21st century who gets in a race with competition, had better be in a jet if that other guy has one.

When you go into a car dealer's showroom today, he assumes you know how to drive his fairly basic vehicle. Limited instruction in operating the car is offered. When you decide to move up to a jet . . . things change. Much more instruction is needed. *TRAINING* in using the better computerized systems will be one of the most important elements . . . if not **the** key ingredient for success . . . with the systems you'll want, Mr. Distributor President. Recognize this, and look for systems that require it. Then, don't become so "penny-wise" with initial cash outlay that you pay for it 100 times over in the decade to come.

Flight Instructor

In a way, the trainers from your new systems firm will act like flight instructors when you're trying to get a pilot's license. They expect that you'll solo after 40 hours of instruction . . . but if you can't, you don't! You must pay for as many hours as the instructor thinks is necessary. You can't be allowed off the ground alone if you're not ready or you'll crash and burn. That's the way it will be with the better computerized systems in the years to come. Only the "instructor" will know when your people are ready to fly alone . . . and you must agree up-front to pay for as many hours as are necessary.

Manufacturers Faced a Similar Problem with MRP

Those of you who've worked in manufacturing at some point in your career may remember when MRP . . . Material Requirements Planning . . . was first introduced into the company. Here comes this computerized-approach to planning the shop production scheduling and material needs, which replaced the thought-process and control of a shop foreman who'd done the job for 25 years. How well was the new concept accepted? The shop foreman loved it . . . right? No way. He hated it! He fought it tooth and nail. No computer was going to take over *his* job! It was quite a while before he absorbed enough training to make the concept work. It was quite a while before he even tried to learn.

Job security is often a major (hidden) issue when you attempt to put any new system of control in place . . . especially when the "system" threatens to replace the logic as to how a person does their job. This is true when you try to let Order Points, Line Points, EOQ's, Review Cycles and all that other new stuff guide a buyer's ordering decisions. "Hey," he or she thinks, "I've been doing the buying around here for 10 years. I've done pretty well using my own judgement. The salesmen like the results. We don't need any new computerized mumbo-jumbo telling *me* how to do my job!"

Do you see why Training in this scene will be both a long project and difficult to apply? Do you understand why I say that only the trainers . . . the flight instructors . . . will know when this company with this buyer is ready to fly with the new controls? The buyer fears a bit for his job. In the past no one really understood exactly how he did the buying. He was valuable. The company needed him. If this new system goes in, other people *will* understand how he's supposed to buy. His performance is measurable. It's discomforting. He wouldn't mind at all if the whole thing failed and the boss threw it out.

Training for this outfit will have to be administered carefully, slowly, by skilled teachers who are good "reassurers" and "convincers," rather than the old-fashioned installer types who taught mechanical steps only. Mr. Distributor President, don't negotiate so hard on the total cost of your new system that you wind up short-changed in this vital training phase. In the future, training will make or break your new system.

Remember the Recovery Room after Surgery

There's another aspect to this need for slow, careful, precise training that borders on counseling at times. Do you remember the last time you or someone you know had major surgery? How many "attendants" hovered around you when you woke up in the recovery room? At least one at all times, and sometimes several. What for? Why didn't they just cart you straight back to your room and serve a hot meal?

Your body's system has undergone major trauma . . . major shock. In those first hours afterward, very close and special care is needed. Your body functions are all out of whack. You've been cut on. The body doesn't react well to that. The ICU nurses need to be right there to help you back to some semblance of order . . . and who decides when you can be taken back to your room? The nurses. If blood pressure, heart rate, temperature, bleeding, shock, or anything else doesn't come back into normal ranges . . . you stay where you are.

It's Like That with a New System Implant

When you apply new Inventory Controls to your company's system, you throw the whole company metabolism into shock. You've cut away the familiar and replaced it with an "implant." The body may try to reject this foreign matter. This is especially true with "Grahamology" where entire operating philosophies are changed in addition to simple job mechanics.

Don't negotiate away the Recovery Room "nurses" you're going to need after the new system is first installed. You need much more help in those first few days and weeks than you'll need later . . . but the training cost is high. So is the Intensive Care Unit. You wouldn't think of telling your doctor:

"Hey listen, Doc. This operation is going to be very expensive. I'd like to save money wherever I can. I don't really have to have an anesthesiologist in surgery, and just take me straight back to my room when you're through. Let's cut out all that intensive care expense."

Talk about painful surgery . . . and you're **really** endangering your life by skipping the recovery room. Fortunately, you can't bargain with the doctor like that. He backs clear away from the whole process if you do. Don't do too much bargaining about training with the systems company who'll install your next software package. You need the nurses while you're recovering, and they alone will know when you're able to begin to make it on your own.

The Systems House Becomes Your Consultant

The better systems houses in the future will need an "open-ended" training contract. They know how your people must perform to get the most from their system . . . but they *don't* know how well your people will take to the training required. Some will learn willingly and easily. Others may drag their feet when they see decisions now made by the computer that they used to make . . . a bit of a job-security threat. Still others may just be incapable of digesting all the confusing new steps, disciplines, and features.

You Have to Trust Somebody

Such an open-ended cost arrangement is naturally repugnant to a distributor executive. It sounds dangerous. The software company could take advantage of the situation . . . but you must trust somebody here. If you thought enough of the package to have signed-up, you must trust the systems installers and trainers. They won't be in business long if they run up the total training bill unnecessarily. Certainly you should talk to other users who've been through the exercise, but *DON'T* try to negotiate out this kind of training help from the contract. You'll pay many times more than the cost in the years to come as the system limps along . . . delivering half of the promised benefits, or you may even crash and burn! You can't afford either result.

LET'S MOVE ON . . . AGAIN

OK, now it's time to get down to Inventory Control business. You've heard all the warnings about computer-selection hazards, the need for in-depth training, and the new attitudes to be adopted about inventory dollars. Let's now discuss some inventory management specifics. Let's talk about areas the first books covered lightly or not at all. These next chapters expand, explain, interpret, and add to the basic control concepts with which (hopefully) you're already familiar. If these next subjects are totally new to you, you should read first: "Distribution Inventory Management For The 1990's," before trying to digest the material that follows here.

Seasonal Items . . .
Forget the Rules!

4

It's Easy to Leave Something Out When Writing a Book

I'm now going to reveal a deep dark secret of authors
. . . especially those who write books for business areas: When you
offer your first material to the market, you're concerned that no
one'll be interested. Which of your ideas will be well-received, if
any, and how much detail should be provided? You probably recall
your old economics textbook from college which served well as a
sure cure for insomnia. Reading a chapter was pure drudgery. A
business author worries (or at least he should) about publishing
something like that.

So in my first efforts to expound a "system" of Inventory Management for distributors, I covered some topics too lightly. To
avoid an encyclopedia of 1000 pages which no one would have read
for sure, I hit highpoints only . . . but in doing this, some critical
warnings and exceptions were omitted. One of these incomplete
topics was seasonal items. So with that explanation and an apology,
let's jump on that slippery subject now.

DEFINITION: SEASONAL ITEM

An item or a product line is often seasonal when 80% of the annual sales volume falls in six months of the year or less. The key word there: "Often." Not every item that fits the definition is seasonal. Some are merely slow-moving, so be careful about applying what I'm about to advise in this chapter. Slow-moving items usually need human-set controls that are frozen by the buyer. Formulas of any breed don't work on the slow-mover . . . the item with usage of less than $1/2$ unit per month (6 per year).

Can the Computer Identify Your Seasonal Items?

Yes . . . it probably can, if you're willing to risk it lumping some items into the seasonal category when they're really just slow-moving. Try this programming approach:

> "OK machine, look back at all stock item histories and locate any item where 80% of the annual activity fell in just six months or less.
>
> Don't list any product with annual usage of less than six units. Likewise, don't list anything we've had in stock less than a year."

Most items the computer finds should be seasonal, but be sure to review the list carefully. Do *not* designate an item as seasonal without a human's approval. The special calculations discussed later on in this chapter will lead to error if the computer categorizes items automatically. The programming limits suggested above might allow some item to slip through incorrectly into the seasonal category . . . but after review, the computer then inserts a seasonal-identifier flag in the records of all approved items.

Frankly, most buyers know the seasonal items quite well. If you have only a limited number, allow the buyers to insert the seasonal-identifier flag into each item's record via a maintenance program. The point: You DO have to identify the seasonal items . . . one way or the other. The computer will then be able to handle them differently from the non-seasonal stock items.

Nearly Every Distributor Has Some Seasonal Products

Likely, you do stock some items that are truly seasonal. Lawn & Garden products have limited appeal in Minneapolis in the Winter but do quite well as Summer approaches. Certain pipe products move fast during the warm construction months up north but slow down when everything freezes up. Portable water coolers for job sites, space heaters, swimming pool products, liners for safety hats . . . all are examples of seasonal items. No one with products like these argues that they're important segments of the business. Trouble is . . . their odd movement patterns present major headaches in ordering them so that there's enough material to begin the season and not much left over when sales slow down. The really crucial time frames are when a season approaches and when it ends.

THE ONE-TIME PURCHASE

Manufacturers often muddy-up the picture by difficult terms under which the seasonal products can be purchased. Yes . . . I know that maybe they *have to* offer the product lines this way to assure year-round production in the factory or to have enough material available to fill all needs in the very short selling season. I'm not being overly critical of the suppliers. I *am* saying that some of these buying requirements make it tough on the distributor.

For example, sometimes you have to buy all your requirements in November for products that don't begin to sell until April. If you wait to order closer to the season, the costs will be much higher . . . if the items are available at all. So the usage forecast for next season must be developed in the Fall for each item. There are only two risks if you're wrong:

1. You could easily run out of several very popular items right in the middle of the season.
2. You could carry a huge overage through the off-season and hope they'll sell next year.

Recovery from either of these pits is expensive. If you must fill-in with an order to the supplier during the season, the costs are 20% higher and the more-popular products are not always available. If you carry-over a big inventory until next year, the carrying costs ("K" Costs . . . remember?) eat up your profits, the merchandise takes up warehouse space, gets damaged or stolen, and next year the supplier changes several models . . . obsoleting your dusty stuff. Buyers ask me once in a while: "How can I get into the consulting business?" One quick way is to make these mistakes on important

seasonal products. You won't have a job. You'll be out here competing with me.

Now you understand why so many ex-buyers for distributors
have ulcers or are committed to state institutions so they can't
harm themselves. When someone tries to outguess the weather,
competition, market conditions, and the economy four to five
months in advance, the odds for success are poor . . . the odds for
a blunder, great.

So Just How Do You Handle a Buying "Opportunity" Like This?

In a word, carefully! First, program the computer to print out all
seasonal items that must be purchased in this manner about one
month before the order must go to the supplier. The listing shows
month-by-month usage for each item by branch back for a year.
Display any trend percentages that have been developed from one
year to the next on an item . . . which means you have at least a
two-year usage pattern.

Next, schedule a meeting with the Sales Manager, Product Manager, or if your company is small, with the entire sales force. Give
them the historical usage plus trend information and let them have a
crack at forecasting what will be sold next season. Separate information is needed, however, for each stock item in each location. General statements are worthless: "You Purchasing people did a poor
job of keeping us in stock on heating repair parts last Fall. You've
sure got to beat that performance next year." How can the Buyers
react to *that,* except by overloading on everything in the category?

The Sales Manager has a tough job admittedly, but his salespeople
are closer to the market and have much more of a feel for what will
happen than anyone else in the company . . . and it must come
down to specific estimates of sales to expect on each item independently during the upcoming season. Statements like, "Boy, we'll
probably sell a lot more of those coolers next Summer" provide no
help. How much of each cooler model and size will sell? That's what
we need. Nobody *likes* to go out on a limb with numbers like this,
but who's better qualified to do the guessing than Sales?

Incentives for Improved Forecasting

Yes, I'm quite aware that most distributor salesmen tend to be overly optimistic when guessing what will happen in the future . . . particularly so if there's no penalty to them personally when actual sales next Summer don't come up to the forecasted numbers. Most salesmen would just as soon see a lifetime supply of everything in the warehouse all the time. Their job is much easier when any item a customer wants is in stock and was purchased at the very lowest cost possible. A variation from either of these conditions forces the salesman out of the "order-taker" and into the "professional" mode. Like most of us, the salesman prefers the easier job.

Stock that sells or doesn't sell still costs about 30 cents per dollar for each year it's in the warehouse. That's the old "K" Inventory Carrying Cost Factor discussed extensively in the 1987 book. Imagine how this cost mounts up on material when you carry it across the off-season with no sales to help turn the investment dollars. So how about this new sales incentive program?

> Mr. Sales Manager, as you forecast sales for next Summer on each item, keep in mind that if any of the inventory we bring in to support this forecast doesn't sell . . . and we can't return it to the supplier, then 1 1/4% of the value will be charged to the Sales Department budget each month we have to carry it across the off-season.

The company absorbs the other 1 1/4% per month. At 30% per year, each month's total carrying cost is 2 1/2%. Sales gets half; the company absorbs the other half. The charges won't be popular. Most negative incentives aren't, but you can bet the salesmen will give a lot more thought, research and effort into the forecasted sales numbers. Remember . . . more distributors fail due to poor asset management (translated here into too much inventory) than for lack of sales.

PURCHASING RIGHT ON THROUGH THE SEASON

Certainly there are seasonal products and product lines that can be purchased right on through the season. You can apply regular inventory controls like Line Points, Order Points and EOQ's, for example, but as the title of this chapter warns . . . forget the normal rules. Adjustments are required.

Be Sure the Computer Uses the Right History to Forecast

The first program modification needed: The time frames from history used to forecast usage on seasonal items in the months just ahead. Instead of the immediate past six months (used for non-seasonal products), the computer looks *ahead* six months using last year's history for the months you're about to enter. If you're at the end of October, the computer reviews:

NOV   DEC   JAN   FEB   MAR   APR

————————— Last Year —————————

The usage numbers recorded for these months for this item in this branch are then averaged. Add them up and divide by six. Remember, some of the histories may have been "overridden." If an override usage is shown in any particular month, that number is the one averaged with the other five . . . rather than the actual usage figure. An override was inserted during last year's season by the buyer if abnormal "one-time" sales were identified for an item, or if you were out of stock for two weeks or more in one of the months being considered . . . and for other reasons as well. An example:

Item: DEF 2610-D   Branch: 10

	NOV	DEC	JAN	FEB	MAR	APR	Average Usage
Actual Usage	26	40	6	58	39	160	40
Override History			30			45	(238 ÷ 6)
			(A)			(B)	

Code A: Out of Stock for More Than Two Weeks

Code B: One-Time Sale of 115 Removed from Consideration

The Seasonal Usage Average Should Be Adjusted

Trends from one year to the next occur on many items, but with non-seasonal products there's no need to modify the simple six-month rolling average other than in *very* extreme trends up or down. The normal calculation at the end of each month, where a new month is added to the averaging and an old one is dropped, takes care of normal growth or decline rates. The averaging begins with last month's data. It's very current.

However, with seasonal items, an adjustment is needed. The usage being averaged begins one year ago. That's pretty dusty information. You should request help from Sales as you approach the new season, and the more specific their answers the better. They may be able to say:

> "On item DEF 2610-D garden hose, we expect to sell 25% more in total this season than last year."
>
> That 40 per month average above is multiplied by 125% = 50
>
> 50 per month is the usage rate the computer will use as we approach the November–April period to compute the Order Point, Line Point, EOQ, etc.

Maybe they can't be that specific, but can provide some general guidelines:

> "We expect to sell about 15% more this year than last on all lawn and garden products."
>
> Every seasonal item in that category now gets a 15% upward adjustment to the usage rate calculated from last year's data.

At worst, you may know only that company sales in total are down 9% this year compared to last. Every seasonal item gets a negative 9% adjustment to last year's usage-average as you prepare to manage inventories for this year's season. Whatever trend information you have . . . specific, general, or very general . . . program the computer to use it to adjust the forecasted usage rates on seasonal items before making the ordering control calculations.

SEASONAL PRODUCT LINES REQUIRE MORE THAN ONE REVIEW CYCLE

Yes, usage rates must be adjusted for seasonal items and so must the product line review cycles. To refresh your memory, the Review Cycle is simply how frequently you place a purchase order with the supplier. Stated another way, it's how often you can get together a $5,000 purchase (for example) of this supplier's products, thereby saving the freight costs . . . without overloading. Problem is, if the product line is seasonal you have to develop two different Review Cycles . . . one to use during the season; one for the rest of the year.

Let's see how to handle a product line where we purchase $100,000 total for the entire year (all 12 months, season and off-season). The supplier requires a $5,000 purchase at cost and then he'll pay the freight. The products are heavy. The $800 freight on a typical order is well worth saving.

$$\frac{\text{Annual Purchases: } \$100,000}{\text{Vendor Requirement: } \$5,000} = 20 \text{ Times per Year}$$

If we divide the required purchase into the total annual purchases, it's easy to see that we can pull an order together about 20 times per year. If the products were non-seasonal, we'd expect to place a P.O. about every two and one-half weeks. A (rounded-up) Review Cycle of three weeks would be just fine. Remember, though, that the products considered here are seasonal. At least 80% of the annual sales take place in just six months or less. Consider a summertime product line like Lawn & Garden supplies:

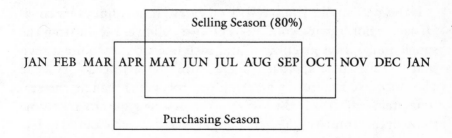

The "Purchasing Season" is also just 26 weeks long. 80% of the annual purchases are made in the March 15–September 15 period. Obviously, we want to begin an inventory buildup before sales actually start and cut back purchases as the season nears its end. Dividing $80,000 by the $5,000 P.O. requirement comes out 16. We can expect to pull together a $5,000 order 16 times . . . but in what time frame? 26 weeks. That develops a Review Cycle of $1\frac{1}{2}$ weeks when we're in the season.

Purchases for the other six months of the year (the off-season) totals $20,000 in our example. We still want the freight paid, so a $5,000 purchase order is still desirable. Dividing $20,000 by $5,000 equals only 4. Only four times during the off-season will we have enough movement in these products to place a $5,000 purchase without overloading. Perhaps we sell a few snow shovels, an occasional snow-blower, etc., which come from the same supplier of lawn & garden equipment . . . but we're located in Oklahoma City. The need for winter-type lawn equipment is not like it'd be in Minneapolis. Four purchases in the six-month off-season would be one approximately every $6\frac{1}{2}$ weeks. (Special Note: A seasonal line out of its season is the only acceptable reason to buy a product less frequently than once a month . . . if you want profit).

Program the Computer to Switch Cycles

In the example above, the computer is programmed to change on March 15th from the out-of-season $6\frac{1}{2}$ week Review Cycle to the $1\frac{1}{2}$ week in-season Cycle and then change the Line Points accordingly for all items in the category. On September 15th, it switches back to the $6\frac{1}{2}$ week Cycle and again changes all Line Points.

Is this perfection? Does it work on every product line every time? Of course not. Buying conditions can vary all over the lot from the simple illustration given here, and each one would require a revision to this whole approach. Experienced buyers need very little assistance like this to set ordering controls which handle the seasonal items effectively. But what if this is a new buyer's first time through this annual cycle? What might you discover about May 1st? The buyer didn't get the inventory buildup started early enough . . . or worse, what might you see on November 15th? Agnes, our new buyer for these products, is still going "hell-bent-for-leather" with P.O.'s. She'll learn not to do this, of course, but at who's expense? Better that the computerized system guides each buyer, experienced or inexperienced, to take the right steps at about the right times.

Accept Less Gross Margin as the Season Draws to a Close

Common sense must always prevail in any purchasing procedure, but sometimes with seasonal items . . . especially in a "Sales-Dominated" distributor . . . personal priorities are allowed to supersede economic sense. Let's say we're coming down to the end of the season on air-conditioning repair parts. It's late August (in the mid-west . . . not Texas, where it's hot until October), and we need to place a $5,000 purchase to keep our low incoming costs. The computer looks ahead to the Fall months as it forecasts usage on each item, of course, so it drops the ordering controls when new calculations are made. We need to buy today. With the suggested buy-quantities dropping, it's going to be really tough to find $5,000 we can buy this time.

If you owned the company, what would you want the buyer to do? Order $750 of the products . . . only those at the critical stage and bring in only enough of each to see us through September. Go ahead and pay the freight. Accept lower gross margins on the sales of this stuff until the season ends.

Why Isn't This OK with Everybody?

Such a common-sense approach is approved by everyone . . . right? Wrong. The salesmen scream loud and long. They're often paid on the gross margin dollars and/or percentages each sale generates. When margins are lower, so are their paychecks. Frankly they're much more interested in what those checks total at the end of the month than how much inventory we might carry across the off-season. In some distributors, the salesmen apply considerable pressure on the buyers to ". . . always get the lowest possible cost from the supplier." As the season winds down, be willing to accept the lower margins. Keep the salespeople off the buyers' backs, and avoid excessive carryover stock from one season to the next. One more time: The Number 1 cause of distributor bankruptcy is mismanaged assets (like inventory). It isn't underpaid salesmen.

ORDER QUANTITY "FENCES"

With non-seasonal products, a distributor following my concepts often uses EOQ (Economic Order Quantity) or perhaps opts for the "Inventory Class" method of computing the quantities to purchase for stock items. Both techniques develop suggested order quantities that are related to the amount of money moving through the inventory. Lot's of money . . . buy smaller quantities and turn the dollars faster. Not much money, buy a lot and turn the dollars slower. This system works very well when the computer is programmed to keep the calculations within certain limits or "fences." It watches for special conditions that call for adjustments to the answers.

Seasonal Conditions Require a Very Important Fence

A surprising (to the Boss) aspect of either EOQ or Inventory Class is that for 50–65% of a distributor's stock items, the formulas suggest buying six months' supply or more at a time. You'll have to read "Distribution Inventory Management For The 1990's" to get more detail about this. It's true and it works *most of the time*. Excellent overall inventory-dollar-turn results, but one of the times you must be very careful with EOQ or Class is when the item is seasonal. It could be pretty silly to buy 11 months' supply of an item, let's say, if it were seasonal and you're almost to the end of the season. EOQ or Class might suggest the large buy if a relatively small number of dollars per year move through the inventory. Neither formula considers the seasonal issue nor where you are right now in the annual cycle of sales.

Limit Suggested Quantities to 3 Months' Supply

You can prevent any serious trouble by programming the computer to limit the suggested order quantity on a seasonal item to 3 months' supply . . . enough to cover the three months you're about to enter right now. For example, you need to purchase a special seal used regularly in heating unit repair. It's only a 40 cent seal. For an entire year, only $36 worth of this seal passes through the inventory. It's a Class 11 item, relative to the dollars going through inventory on other items. The EOQ or Inventory Class formulas advise buying a 10 to 11 months' supply.

But today's date is May 1st. The heating unit repair season is almost over. Buying that much of the seal now is dumb. However, if the computer suggests that you buy only enough seals to meet needs in May, June, and July . . . certainly not very much . . . the recommendation isn't brilliant but it is at least much smarter. Next September, you might be just fine to buy for the whole season, but again the "system" suggests only that you meet the needs expected in October, November and December.

An Experienced Buyer Might Override Either Suggestion

Please don't interpret this 3-month fence as the perfect answer for seasonal items. It isn't. It's purpose is to protect the inexperienced buyer. Some ol' boy who's been buying these heating repair products for 15 years may wisely override either of the 3-month-supply suggestions from our example. In the Spring, he may buy nothing. In the Fall, he buys for the whole season. The 3-month fence does, however, help out Agnes. She's our brand new buyer who's purchasing this product group for the very first time. She's just now beginning to grasp how EOQ's work. She computed one the other day on her hand calculator and was pleased to see that she could get the right answer. Now it's May 1st and the seal needs replenishment. If a normal EOQ is suggested, perhaps 11 months' supply, Agnes likely follows that recommendation to the letter. Later she discovers that buying those seals now was kind of dumb.

No one gets too bent out of shape if a buyer spends $36 a few months early. When Agnes tells her boss what happened, he kids her . . . laughingly . . . until she explains that she did the same thing on 300 other seasonal items. How does Agnes feel *now* about anything else this "stupid computer system" *ever* suggests in the future? "You can't trust the thing!" . . . she says, and her SWAG prevails from here on in. You must be extremely careful that your computerized system *never* suggests that a buyer do something ridiculous. If it does, that buyer may never trust the system again.

The 3-Month Fence Also Serves Well as You Enter a Season

Similarly, the system limits it's suggested order quantity to the next three months' needs even as the season looms just ahead. Consider a product like winter liners for safety hats. It sells very well in Minneapolis in November, December and January. If Agnes places an order in October . . . and she buys only enough to meet those three months' expected requirements, she hasn't made a serious mistake. Oh sure, with experience she might buy enough to last the entire winter season. Next year, we'd expect her to do some "overriding" to these 3-month-limit purchase suggestions . . . but not this year. Not her first year. The computer suggests conservative quantities that keep her in safe waters.

DOUBLE AND SHORT-SEASON PRODUCT LINES

Finally on this subject of seasonality, let's discuss briefly the problem of product lines that have two seasons and others where the selling period is very short. We don't need to spend much time here. There are no brilliant answers.

The Two-Season Product Line

Certain repair parts, and of course many other types, can on occasion meet the seasonal definition (80% of the annual sales in six months or less), but the six months are not consecutive. Three months are in the Spring and three in the Fall. A heat pump/air conditioning unit might have the same part fail when the unit is first turned on in the late Spring . . . and again in the early Fall. Certain plumbing items sell very well all through the construction months in Alaska . . . and again in the dead of winter when those same items freeze up and have to be replaced.

For most products like these, my suggestion is to program your computer to print out a complete list about 30 days ahead of each season start date . . . about March 1st in the Spring, August 1st for the Fall, etc. The buyer then places an order to cover only the immediate season on expensive products . . . but covers both seasons on the inexpensive stuff. The printed list is basically a "Stock Status" (which normally I don't like to use as the basis for buying decisions). In this case, the computer tells you how each item stands. The buyer studies the expected demand in the upcoming season(s) and sends in the order. In my view, trying to calculate computerized guide-lines leads to error when the seasonal problem gets this complicated.

The Short-Season Product Line

I'd use a similar approach with Christmas products and others that have a very brief selling season. Usually, these critters have to be ordered from the supplier in August . . . or at least pretty far ahead of the season . . . and you just hope the sales forecasts are reasonably accurate. The purchase order goes in with your best bet of what will sell on each item. If your guess is short on some fast-selling item, you'll run out about December 10th. If you go too heavy, you may have to move the stuff at 50%-off in January or carry 430 cases over until next year. None of these helps your acid indigestion, but that's the nature of this buying "opportunity." You're disappointed? You were expecting some brilliant formula? Com'on, this requires the purest form of SWAG . . . "Scientific," Wild-Ass Guesswork. Scientific, because your buyer (hopefully) does have a good feel for which products will sell this Christmas, based on sales of these or similar items last year. Guesswork, because all kinds of things could go wrong. Some competitive sup-

plier (whose products you don't carry) brings out a real winner
. . . a "Cabbage-Patch Doll" thing . . . that wipes out the market for anything like it which might have sold just fine last year.
Maybe your items are slightly modified this year, and the customers
don't take to them nearly as well as they did with last year's stuff.

It's a Form of "Craps-Shoot"

With short-season products, you gather as much information as you
can . . . you take your shot . . . and hope it turns out right on
most of the items. You do the same thing in Las Vegas. Hopefully,
the odds are better. Experience is vital and can swing the odds in
your favor. Buyers can develop a very good "feel," as seasons come
and go, for what sells and what doesn't.

SUMMARY

Seasonal items offer several challenging ways to foul up trying to
buy them right, develop solid service levels when sales are hot, and
avoid excessive carryover stocks from one year to the next. Like a
juggler, you have to keep several balls up in the air all the time
. . . but seasonal balls are slippery, odd-shaped, not all the same
weight, and break when they hit the floor. Remember these key
points:

1. Don't expect your regular inventory control system and programming rules to handle seasonal items. Modifications are
   necessary in almost every aspect from forecasting through
   the control calculations all the way to an expanded use of
   SWAG.
2. The computer can identify some seasonal items, but it usually
   makes some mistakes trying. A human always reviews the list
   and makes the final decision as to which items are seasonal;
   which aren't.
3. Seasonal product lines are often purchased with two different
   frequencies: A short cycle during the season . . . a longer
   cycle the rest of the year.

4. Limit the computer's suggested order quantities to "the next three months' needs" when items are seasonal. It isn't a perfect answer, but it protects the new buyer and prevents your system from suggesting something stupid.

5. Two-Season and Short-Season products offer a golden opportunity to refine your SWAG. Nothing else but experience works very well.

Now . . . if you think seasonal items present a hazard, you're starting to get much smarter. You're becoming aware of the what's required in a computerized system to do a solid job for the wholesale distributor. You've just begun. The next chapters deal with branches, centralized warehousing and the like. My suggestion is to go ahead right now and find the Excedrin (or Valium) bottle. These next subjects may increase your pain or nerve disorders.

Central Warehousing . . . Is It the Answer for Multi-Branch Distributors?

5

A hot topic these days is the merit of consolidating stocks in a central warehouse for redistribution to smaller branches. Is it better to keep only the slow-movers in the warehouse? Should you keep just the popular items there? How much of a product line spread is really necessary at branch level? What will local customers say when they can't get every item in every size immediately? Should the branches buy for themselves . . . or is that better done centrally by someone aware of conditions throughout the company or region? Can you use the same controls in a branch for ordering decisions that work in the central warehouse?

The popularity of centralized vs. decentralized operation seems to cycle as the years go by. Everyone moves toward the centralized approach for a while . . . then it seems better to move back toward more autonomous branches. The factors which can guide you to the preferred mode change as the economic scene changes, as employees come and go, and as the company grows or shrinks.

You may be surprised to learn that it really doesn't matter which way you function if you fit the conditions necessary to make that setup work. Much more important are the answers to several basic questions: Is your company sales "dominated" or sales "oriented"? How do pay scales motivate your managers and salesmen? What are the skill levels of your purchasing people at the home office and in the branches? Are there disciplines in your company and accuracy in the information generated? What's the real capability of your computerized system? Are you a fearful or confident president?

THE BASIC PRINCIPLES

For a moment, though, let's state a simple principle that guides how a product line, an item, or all items should be handled . . . centralized or decentralized:

> If a branch can buy directly from a supplier, get the same competitive cost the warehouse or central buyer can achieve, and doesn't have to overload the shelves in the process . . . buy direct! Don't involve anyone else in the decision making, ordering, expediting, and receipt. If that can't be done without overloading the stock; if the central warehouse can buy better and not have the savings eaten away by redistribution expense . . . then the central approach is the way to go.

THE MORE FUNDAMENTAL CONSIDERATIONS

It would be nice if it really were that simple. It isn't. Unfortunately, the overriding "IF" lurking in the basic principle above is: "**. . . without overloading the stock.**" By who's definition? How much is too much? What ground-root-level factors have an impact on how much stock winds up in a branch . . . no matter how carefully you select the way it *should be* handled?

For example, salesmen in the branch want every item in a product line carried in local stock, in unlimited quantity. Their opinion of "too much" is invalid, but how much weight do they carry in your company? Are you sales "dominated"? Many distributors are. How about your branch managers? What are their real feelings about inventory size? A properly-motivated branch manager, paid partially on how much inventory is carried, doesn't allow overloads . . . but a "sales-dominated" manager who feels no pressure about inventory levels (other than an occasional irate call

from the controller) needs the restraint of someone centrally making his major stock-replenishment decisions.

HAVE YOU EVALUATED YOUR PURCHASING PROFESSIONALISM?

Skill levels of the purchasing personnel play a role in deciding the operating mode to adopt. What if only two people (both in the home office) in your company *really* understand effective inventory management concepts, controls, and disciplines. Only these two have grasped thoroughly how your new computerized purchasing system works . . . have pushed themselves to learn all the latest new stuff and move away from SWAG . . . while most of the people in the branches haven't or won't. You don't need a consultant to know which mode is better for YOU! The Purchasing function for your branches will prove more profitable when moved back into the hands of the two skilled buyers until more skills can be developed in (or hired for) the branches.

RECORD ACCURACY MUST BE CONSIDERED

People removed physically from a stocking location can make effective ordering decisions, at the right time and in the right quantities, only when the information they use is very accurate. The computer says that the Des Moines branch is down to 6 pieces on an important stock item. It shows that Des Moines sells about 10 per month. If these are right . . . a remote buyer back in the central warehouse can have replenishment stock arrive in Des Moines without much risk of a stockout.

But what if neither of these numbers is any good? Some sales for the item have been misposted and the shelf count in Des Moines is actually 26 due to sloppiness in paperflow or material processing? Does this sound like one of your branches? If so, it's crippling to profit . . . but you might as well leave the ordering decisions at branch level until the problems are corrected. Someone there must go into the warehouse to check stock before making a replenishment decision. The remote guy would make too many incorrect decisions based on the computer's data.

DECISIONS ON WHERE TO POSITION
STOCK ITEMS

It's important to have your stock in the right places. Pretty hard to argue with that sage piece of wisdom . . . but distributors historically (or maybe hysterically) allow big chunks of their inventory

dollars to remain in dark, dank out-of-the-way . . . so to speak
. . . locations. Again, a basic principle should be applied:

> Keep the bread, milk, eggs and cheese at branch level right next to the
> customer and available on demand. Keep the imported Bolivian an-
> chovies back at the Central Warehouse, available to any one of the
> branches within a day or two.

Hopefully you realize I'm not talking about food here. You have
products with similar popularity ranges. Just keep in mind, this
WILL NOT receive the approval of your salespeople out in the
branches! They like to keep "show" stock at the local level. A salesman fusses: "What if a customer came in here and didn't see Item
28J up there on our shelf. He might think we're going out of business on that group of products!" Your reply: "Well, we don't sell but
one or two a year . . . sometimes none at all for 16 months. Do we
want to have stock around here for *show* ?" The salesman (regardless
of how he answers) is thinking "Sure!"

You're Not in Show Business

Are you in "Show Business?" Madonna . . . yes. Michael Jackson
. . . yes. Distributors . . . NO! You're in the profit-making business. The Number 1 cause of distributor bankruptcy is *too much
inventory!* (Are you getting this message?) You can't afford very
much "show" stock. Often I see distributors carry 3, 2, 2, 6, 4, and
7 of a slow-moving item in six branches and then also in the Central
Warehouse . . . when none in the branches and 5 in the warehouse
would have met every demand for the item over the last year with
only a one-day lag in delivery. OK . . . one item like this wouldn't
make all that much difference in the total inventory dollars carried
across the year. What if you have 4000 like this however?

SALES DOMINATION VS. SALES ORIENTATION

Why do salesmen raise such a stink about this? Most distributors
are sales "dominated" . . . not sales "oriented." This has been
mentioned several times thus far in the book, but what does it

mean? Salesmen call all the shots. Salespeople in the branches threaten to quit if the manager doesn't stock what they specify in the quantities they want. Just remember the mourning period for one of these salesmen if you do in fact go bankrupt. It's just two days. First day . . . he plays golf. Second day . . . he's got a job with your competitor. He knows the products and (if you're out of business because of poor asset control) he brings customers with him.

WHAT MOTIVATES YOUR SALESMEN?

This sounds like I've got it in for salespeople. I don't. I'd have the same attitude if I worked for most distributors . . . maybe for you. You pay me on the gross margin dollars and percentages I generate. My job is easier if you carry an item in local stock and bought it at the very lowest cost possible from the supplier. If it isn't on the shelf here in my branch . . . or if you didn't get the lowest cost . . . my job is more difficult. Much more professionalism is required in my selling skills. I'd have to move up from an order-taker who sells only on price . . . to a professional who can still get the order when my preferences about local stock are not in the best interests of the company's long-range business health.

Sales Compensation Methods *Do* Affect Inventory Attitudes

Am I making too much of this? Is this really important in deciding what items will be stocked and where? Consider again the basic pay motivation for a salesman. When a slow-moving stock item finally sells after 11 months, the salesman generates a full markup . . . 28% margin, perhaps. His commission is based on the gross margin dollars and percent. He's happy.

A more profitable method for handling the item would have been *NOT* to carry it in stock all that time . . . but make the sale (when one finally occurred) by going by the competitor or a local warehouse on a buyout basis and delivering to the customer. True . . . the gross margin percent would be only 12% rather than 28% . . . but what did you avoid for 11 months? . . . and what's the Number 1 cause of distributor bankruptcy?

The salesman objects if you handle it that way. His pay is cut or non-existent. He isn't compensated on such low margins. He doesn't care if an item stays on your shelf until it reaches antique status. If and when he finally does sell it, he makes full compensation. Besides . . . what does he care how big your inventory is? It costs him nothing except in the will-o-the-wisp profit sharing at year-end, and no one lets that incomprehensible calculation affect his monthly pay.

Now do you understand why you have all those odd-ball items out in the branches (and maybe in the main branch also)? Any move to reposition significant numbers of these critters . . . carry no stock at all at branch level and less centrally, with a delay in shipping to any remote customer . . . or to drop "dog" class items entirely from stock . . . might cause a riot, unrest, bloodshed, mutiny, or bodily threats from your sales force. What's the answer? A whole new concept of salesmen's pay, wherein they're motivated to sell an item the *best way,* at perhaps a lower margin if the overall profit result at year end would be better. Why not work on **that** before going central?

THEN THERE'S YOUR GUT CHECK

How's your Management intestinal fortitude? Do you develop your "game plan" to win . . . regardless of individual biases or preferences? That plan must certainly make the most of the skill levels of key players, but it cannot accommodate a poor work ethic or short sightedness from anyone. There are still distributor presidents . . . more than there should be in today's business climate . . . who're afraid of their salesmen. "Some of my best guys might quit if I make major changes in where we stock the items they want!" If your sales force holds *you* hostage, you're like a football coach afraid to call a pass play for fear that the all-pro right guard might not like having to block his opponent . . . whom he doesn't seem to be able to handle today. The decisions to position stock in a central warehouse, in only one branch, or at the all branches are "coach level" decisions. My point? *YOU* must run your company in a manner most conducive to long-range business health! If you don't . . . or can't . . . it won't matter whether you're centralized or decentralized.

ANOTHER HAZARD . . . AN IMPROPER ATTITUDE TOWARD BRANCHES IN A CENTRAL MODE

One final hangup must be avoided if you think a central distribution center is the way you should go. What's the attitude in the home office (often the original and largest branch) about those people in the branches? If you decide to resupply them from a central point, would you *really* treat them and their needs as you do customers today?

I see distributors all the time in a centralized warehousing environment make the home office branch manager responsible for the warehousing operations. This guy is paid basically on sales to local customers, just as he has been for 15 years. Now *his* warehouse people have been beefed up a bit and, yes, there may be more space in *his* new warehouse . . . but his pay isn't affected one way or the other by how he serves the branches. So guess how they're served? When there's not enough stock to fill everyone's requirements, guess who gets it? The branches soon get a clear message: You're second class!

How do they react? The same way you would. They put no trust at all in the central warehouse to take care of them. They stock large quantities of every-thing; all manner of odd-ball items; go with any brand they can get . . . and your central warehousing plan turns into a disaster.

WHAT'S THE RIGHT APPROACH

The manager of your central warehouse must view requirements from the branches as if they were coming from customers . . . because, when you really think about it, they are! Indirectly, it's true, but the branch needs for stock represents needs from their customers. This warehouse manager is paid on his overall performance. He must take care of local customers, but he must *also* have a very high service level performance to the branches. At times, he may have to say "No" to the local branch manager's customer backorder in favor of stock for a branch.

"Heresy!," you scream. "Impossible!" "Graham, you're crazy!" You'd better listen if you want central distribution to work and generate the anticipated benefits of lower overall inventories and improved service.

SO WHAT'S THE ANSWER TO THE BIG QUESTION

This chapter hasn't answered it's own question: "Is Centralized Warehousing the answer for most multi-branch distributors?" . . . and it can't. That decision must be preceded by a difficult self-evaluation of factors deeply-rooted in each distributor's old habits, professionalism (or lack thereof) with Sales and Purchasing personnel, buying power with suppliers, computer record accuracy, degree of sales domination, compensation methods, computer system capabilities, attitudes about branch needs vs. a local customer, and management style. What's right for the guy in the next state may be wrong for you. Just as a football team must work on basics . . . blocking and tackling . . . before deciding that their offense will be built around running or passing, so does the distributor.

You'd better evaluate and correct your basics too, before deciding that you want a centralized or decentralized operation. How are your salesmen paid? Do branch managers have incentives to keep a low inventory . . . other than threats from the home office? Are your records accurate as to quantities in stock . . . or would you find 40 out of 100 to be off if you ran a spot check? What's the professional skill level of your purchasing managers and buyers? How many still make decisions by guesswork? Are your salesmen price cutters and order-takers rather than true professionals who want the company to prosper? Does your

Frankly, are you equipped to run a truly centralized operation . . . or any other mode in an effective manner? When you know that your basics are sound . . . when you know (and have corrected) the attitudes and skill levels of your personnel . . . when you have the right computerized system for your size and distributor type . . . .you'll know the answer to which mode is better for you! When you have the basics down . . . and you still don't know . . . sell the company. Someone'll get a super buy.

Branch Operations . . . Revisited

6

OK . . . you've analyzed your operation, developed the right professionals in the right places, moved more into a sales-oriented mode, become an aggressive president, developed new pay plans for salesmen and managers . . . and you decide to operate in a centralized warehousing environment. You've established a large central or regional warehouse which is expected to supply the needs of several satellite branches. Now what? How should it function? What're the best ways to assure the lowest overall inventory . . . but a very good level of customer service in all locations?

You can make a lot of money if you structure a central or regional warehouse to do its job well. You can lose a bundle . . . and wish you'd never attempted the change . . . if you don't. Since computers now play such a vital role with distributors, and since better software has been developed in the last few years . . . there are now options in central warehouse operations that just weren't practical even five years ago.

Branches Offer Another Hazard in Software

Unfortunately, there's far too much software offered to distributors today that does an abominable job of handling branch resupply in a centralized mode. I'm not sure why. Perhaps it's because the software was developed initially for a single-branch distributor . . . then taken to the market. Very quickly it was apparent that the package must adapt to multi-branch distributors, and so "branch-handling" was added. The modifications were "driven" entirely by the first company needing the additional features. The software people really didn't know what was right or wrong. They just built the system as instructed.

Watch Out for Missing Features

One of the often-omitted features is the software's capability to allow branches to be resupplied under the "Push" concept. Another is the ability to post usage histories correctly through "Replenishment Path Codes." Both were discussed in "Distribution Inventory Management For The 1990's" but with coverage that was a little too light. More discussion is needed:

- For a full understanding of how these techniques work
- To be sure your computer is programmed properly to handle several resupply variations
- To be sure you get *all* the benefits possible from your branch inventory investments, and . . .
- To be sure you don't buy some software outfit's "Me, Too" package which can't do any of this stuff.

To begin, let's get back into the "Push" method of resupplying branches from a central warehouse.

"PUSH" VERSUS THE OLD RELIABLE "PULL" METHOD

When an outlying branch needs resupply of a stock item, drawn from a "mother" warehouse, you can always fall back on old reliable . . . the "Pull" method. Nothing happens until the branch decides more stock is needed. What follows is simple and basic: They contact somebody at the warehouse by fax, phone or mail to get the replenishment process started. The next day, or maybe just once a week, the replenishment shipment arrives from "mother."

The branch monitors their own inventory status. The branch decides how much to transfer in. They also decide when to do it. That's the old "Pull" method of warehouse/branch resupply. The branch pulls from the central warehouse whatever they need, whenever they need it. Action is initiated by the branch. Oh sure . . . the computer is part of the process, but it's used only to warn the branch that stock on an item is running low. It then waits for someone locally to take action.

There Are Many Variations

In your company, or for a particular item, the steps may vary slightly. The central warehouse doesn't actually maintain stock from which the branch pulls what they need. Instead, the warehouse merely orders all branch requirements from the supplier at the same time a purchase order is placed for warehouse needs. Material may be shipped directly to the branch from the supplier, or it may come in to the warehouse to be redistributed immediately. The branch knows the ordering schedule or is alerted when a P.O. is about to be placed. The warehouse really isn't that at all. It acts as an "order-accumulator."

Regardless of the variation, the reason a distributor elects to function like this is also quite basic: The central warehouse or order-accumulator can buy in quantity. The branch can't. By working through the warehouse, branches enjoy "truckload" pricing on their material . . . and the cost of redistribution doesn't offset the savings. Branches operate with much lower inventories, turning faster, than would be possible if each attempted to buy directly from the supplier. The warehouse inventories . . . in that mode where stocks are maintained for branch use . . . turn more slowly, but again, the costs involved are offset by higher turns in the branches. The Pull method is as old as the hills. It's been around in one form or the other since the first distributor set up his first branch.

Disadvantages of the Pull Method

Any corporate inventory manager, or president, who's worked in the "Pull" environment has a complaint: "Boy, it's tough to get the branch managers to keep their inventories down. Those turkeys tend to load up their shelves!" True. They do. Why? . . . because most distributors are still sales "dominated," rather than sales "oriented." Taking care of the customer (at *any* cost) is their goal. That job is easier when there's a lifetime supply of every item out in the warehouse. Most branch managers were once (and maybe still are) salesmen. They think like salesmen . . . not like money managers, which is now their primary role.

Pay Plans Get Blamed Again

The branch managers' pay plan contributes to their attitude. Most are paid on "operating" profit . . . the difference between gross margin dollars generated and costs of running the branch. There's no cost, in these numbers at least, for the inventory dollars carried. Inventory is considered an asset . . . not a cost. Oh sure, once in a while the president gets on a manager's case about how much inventory he has, but there's no real penalty. The manager's pay is unaffected. The manager isn't stupid. He **knows** that it's easier for his salesmen to sell when the shelves are full than when they're on the lean side. . . . and he knows how he's paid. So do the salesmen.

Under the "Pull" approach, the manager controls when and how much material is ordered for replenishment. He has little interest in keeping inventories down. His branch functions better, he reasons, and his pay reflects it when the shelves are jammed. His salesmen don't gripe as much; the phone doesn't ring with a problem as often. Life is easier.

You Must Force Higher Inventory Turn Rates in the Branches

When managers think along these lines, Top Management needs to remove much of the "stock level" decision-making from their control. You must force the branch inventories down so that they'll turn faster than any form of Pull resupply would develop. For most durable goods distributors, 5 to 6 pure turns with a sales gross margin range of 20 to 30% generates solid profits *in the warehouse*. The same margins require 8 to 10 turns for adequate profits in a branch. 12 turns per year would be even better, and it's attainable if you apply the right controls.

The Branch Needs to Pay Back Something for the Array of Services Received

It's only logical. A branch receives the benefits of several corporate services (Accounting, Personnel, Benefits, etc.), a large warehouse inventory, and special delivery conditions that would not be enjoyed if they stood alone as an independent entity. True, they get hit with a "corporate services" charge each month, but in most companies this doesn't even approach the real costs. The branch **SHOULD** perform at a higher gross margin dollar-per-employee ratio and a higher inventory turn rate!

Why the higher turns? For most items, they have no "Line Buy" to contend with. They can replenish one item at a time. They can bring in one unit, two, or whatever, without a unit cost penalty . . . in fact, even low quantities like this still enjoy the volume discounts secured by the warehouse. It's logical that the inventory investment should turn more rapidly than in the warehouse. The Min/Max controls for each branch must reflect your company's turnover objectives. Since that's true . . . the setting of these replenishment controls should be assigned to someone more objective than the branch manager.

THE "PUSH" METHOD OF SETTING BRANCH REPLENISHMENT CONTROLS

Computer capability today allows a different approach entirely to how branch inventories are controlled. Rather than allowing a branch to "pull" material from the warehouse when, and in the quantity they want . . . the merchandise rather is "pushed" out to them in accord with the company's turnover objectives. The computer controls, in effect, the inventory levels for items resupplied out of the central warehouse. By removing this function from local branch control, a much higher inventory-dollar turn is generated over the course of a year. As I said, you should target 12 turns per year!

Be Sure to Do Your Homework before Starting

There are prerequisites . . . conditions, that must be present in your company for the "push" method to work:

1. As discussed in the last chapter, the central warehouse views the needs from branches (to be supported from its inventory) on the same level with customers. The warehouse manager is paid on overall service performance to both local customers and branches. Branches *are not* treated as orphans.

2. The computer is updated nightly. The balance shown as available for sale for each stock item in each branch and in the central warehouse is recomputed every evening after posting all sales, transfers, receipts, returns, and cycle counts in all company locations. (This might be done "on-line," of course, where balances change with each transaction keyed . . . but you must at least update the balances nightly.)

3. These balances must be very accurate. Each company location works in the "Day's-Work-In-A-Day" environment, as regards paperwork and material flow . . . and has an effective Cycle Count program underway. We'll talk more about Cycle Counting in the next chapter.

4. The computer has the capability, and has been programmed, to develop simple usage rates, minimums, and maximums at least once a month . . . using the sales histories for each stock item in each branch.

Next . . . An Item Classification

Each stock item in each branch is assigned a "movement-class." Class 1 items are those with the most dollars moving through that branch's inventory in a year; Class 12 items have the least dollars;

Class 13 items are the dogs. Each item has a class assigned . . . from 1 through 13. The details for this classification step are given in "Distribution Inventory Management For The 1990's!" As with a number of subjects in this book, the earlier one provides necessary background to help you understand my points here.

An Item's Class Dictates Its Inventory Turnover Objective

If a branch inventory is to turn 12 times per year in total, then the Class 1 items must turn even faster . . . 20 times a year. The objectives would look like this:

Class 1 — 20 times per year	Class 7 — 8 times per year
Class 2 — 18 times per year	Class 8 — 6 times per year
Class 3 — 16 times per year	Class 9 — 4 times per year
Class 4 — 14 times per year	Class 10 — 3 times per year
Class 5 — 12 times per year	Class 11 — 2 times per year
Class 6 — 10 times per year	Class 12 — 1 times per year

90% of all the money moving through the branch's inventory in a year will be found in the Class 1 through 4 items, but they're only 35% of the total number stocked. Only 10% of the annual money-movement will be in the Class 5 through 12 items . . . but they'll be 65% of the total number stocked.

Branches Need Only Basic Replenishment Controls

Very simple replenishment controls are needed for a branch stock item when resupply comes from a central warehouse. When the stock reaches a "Minimum," the warehouse ships a quantity to bring it up to a "Maximum." The old "Min/ Max" type controls work quite well when lead time is short and the supplier (in this case a "mother" warehouse) is reliable. Both are true here. The branch can be resupplied at least weekly . . . perhaps overnight in an emergency. The warehouse maintains a stock to "buffer" the branch from the longer lead times and unreliability of outside suppliers: the manufacturers from whom the warehouse buys. The branch deals with a very reliable supplier. It needs very simple replenishment controls only.

An Item's Class Now Helps to Set Its "Maximum"

We'll talk about the "Minimum" calculation a little later on. Right now, let's discuss the "Maximum." The computer tracks a branch stock item's condition each evening. When it drops to the "Minimum," the computer adds the item to the next transfer from the central warehouse stock to the branch. The quantity to be sent is the difference between the item's "Minimum" and "Maximum," as follows:

Class 1 —	$1/20$th of a year's supply	2.5 weeks' supply (Approx.)	
Class 2 —	$1/18$th "	3 week's	"
Class 3 —	$1/16$th "	3.5 week's	"
Class 4 —	$1/14$th "	4 week's	"
Class 5 —	$1/12$th "	1 month's	"
Class 6 —	$1/10$th "	5.5 week's	"
Class 7 —	$1/8$th "	6.5 week's	"
Class 8 —	$1/6$th "	8.5 week's	"
Class 9 —	$1/4$th "	3 months'	"
Class 10 —	$1/3$rd "	4 months'	"
Class 11 —	$1/2$ "	6 months'	"
Class 12 —	1 Year's supply	1 year's	"
Class 13 —	Not Resupplied		

Inventory Turns Are Forced

The computer knows how much of each item is being sold per year . . . either from past sales histories or forecasts. It's no trick to divide this annual usage by the proper number above, round the answer off to standard pack, and print out a picking ticket to get that quantity transferred out to the branch. Inventory turnover is removed from branch control. The branch doesn't order replenishment material when and in the quantity it chooses . . . the "Pull" method. Rather, the material is "Pushed" out to the branch in accord with branch inventory status, corporate turnover objectives, sales patterns, and controls developed from all three.

"How Can We Be Sure We Won't Run out of Stock?"

The "Minimum" acts as the replenishment-*timing* trigger. It keeps the branch from running out of stock. The **quantities** transferred from the warehouse determine what dollar inventory turn will result. The Minimum has plenty of safety stock built into its calculation and, like the Maximum, is refigured by the computer each month.

How to Calculate a "Minimum"

The Minimum is very similar to an Order Point, but with two important variations. The formula:

$$\text{Minimum} = (\text{Usage Rate} \times \text{Lead Time}) + \text{Safety Allowance}$$

The Usage Rate is the rate of sale per month the branch experiences on a stock item, calculated just as the warehouse does on one of their items. However, Lead Time may be set and locked-in as 1 Week, and the Safety Allowance percentage may also be locked-in at 50%. Back in the warehouse, Lead Time and Safety Allowance vary all over the lot, but not so in a branch . . . when resupply is from "mother."

Remember . . . the warehouse acts as a "buffer" for a branch between them and an erratic outside source with lead times that bounce all around . . . a source who also may require truckload purchases to get good prices. The branch may draw any quantity needed from the central warehouse. No large purchases required, and they can get it very quickly. Replenishment for an item with low stock can often occur in one day's time. The worst delay is probably only a week. The regularly-scheduled replenishment truck arrives each Tuesday. One week's lead time may be set for every item resupplied from "mother." 50% is enough safety for the same basic reasons. The branch has a very reliable source for their stock resupply. The buffer inventory carried in the warehouse assures the branch of excellent continuity of supply. The safety allowance is needed only to protect against variations in usage.

The Procedure for Seasonal Items

Even after that earlier chapter on seasonal items, we're still not through with those critters. Here's *another* condition involving seasonal products that requires different computer system programming. It would be pretty dumb to send a branch five months' supply of a winter liner for safety hats in May. Where you are in the year, compared to a product's season *must* be considered in determining how much of an item to send in replenishment. Also for seasonal items, you wouldn't want to send 12 months' supply (for example) of anything out to a branch . . . regardless of the item's movement class.

Seasonal products make the "Push" procedure more complex . . . perhaps too much so for any form of automatic computerized replenishment. You likely should opt to handle them with more personal control all through the year. One buyer in the warehouse may have to be assigned to "ride herd" on a particular line of seasonal products for all company locations . . . watching the branch sales patterns, refiguring the controls, and deciding personally how much to send a branch on the next truck.

Record Accuracy Is Mandatory for Push to Work

If this key prerequisite is missing . . . accurate records in the computer of what the branch actually has on the shelves . . . then forget the Push concept. It'd be a disaster. Branches would receive merchandise they didn't need and not receive stuff when they're out. Cycle Counting must be a way of life. You must remove the errors created by all those mis-steps or mistakes in paperwork or material handling, general sloppiness, theft, misfilled orders, kits broken into, salesmen removing samples without paperwork . . . you know what goes on in your company. The computer balances *must* be accurate.

Accurate balances are the responsibility of each branch manager. For that reason, all transactions involving the branch should be input into the computer *out at the branch!* The branch keys their own sales orders; receipts; returns; and cycle count adjustments. None of this is done for them back at the corporate office or at the regional warehouse. The "Day's-Work-In-A-Day" standard is the branch manager's responsibility. Nobody buys it when he says: "Heck, our records are all fouled up because you people at the home office didn't get our paperwork keyed-in correctly or on time!" Sorry, Mr. Manager. If your records stink . . . it's because **YOU** didn't do your job at the branch. You went home with work undone. You didn't cycle count. The responsibility for accuracy, completeness, timeliness is *your's!* It's a measure of your job performance.

REPLENISHMENT PATH CODES

Chapter 16 of *Distribution Inventory Management For The 1990's* introduced you to the concept of Replenishment Path codes inserted into your computerized system to make sure usage gets posted to the proper branch when material moves between company locations. Before reading this section, you'd do well to review the material in that earlier book on branch operations.

The path code is not a commandment . . . only a recommendation. Let's say that our Long Beach branch expects to be resupplied on item # DEF 2610 from our large Central Warehouse in Los Angeles. A code in the computer file for DEF 2610 in Long Beach designates this Los Angeles/Long Beach replenishment path. Note several rules about the path:

1. Long Beach never brings in material from outside the company if Los Angeles has stock. They *do not have* the option of buying direct from the supplier **OR** transferring in material from another branch when L.A. has stock available to take care of their needs.

2. Long Beach does try to transfer-in material from some other company location if L.A. is temporarily unable to fill their

replenishment need on item DEF 2610. If they can, the usage is *still posted in Los Angeles* . . . and not in the branch from whom they got the stock.

3. If no other branch can help and Long Beach has to go outside the company to buy material, the amount purchased is again shown as usage in Los Angeles.

These rules aren't intended as arbitrary restraints placed on the poor Long Beach branch to make life miserable. It's true that nobody likes them very much since they won the company's annual bowling tournament last Summer and then danced around screaming: "We're Number 1 !" Their little demonstration in the end zone after winning the flag football game at the picnic didn't set well either, but none of this is the purpose for tying them down like this. The rules are just common sense.

Los Angeles Must Prepare for *Something*

The Los Angeles warehouse has been assigned the responsibility to take care of Long Beach stocking needs on item DEF 2610. What would happen if the next time Long Beach needs replenishment, they buy direct from the supplier . . . but the time after that, they draw stock from L.A.? How would L.A. ever know what to expect? What should they protect for? What inventory level should they maintain to be sure they can take care of Long Beach and all the other branches as well?

That's the reason for Rule Number 1 above. "Hey, Long Beach, once Top Management decides that replenishment for you on item DEF 2610 is to come from Los Angeles . . . that's it. If they have stock, you *always* get it there." Los Angeles counts on the usage. They expect it. They build inventories to protect for Long Beach needs. They *don't* get left out to dry with a big stock because Long Beach, this time, decided to go direct. They *don't* also show declining usage . . . since Long Beach didn't draw the stock . . . and drop their inventory, only to have Long Beach expect resupply the next time. Imagine 20,000 items in Los Angeles put there to take care of ten branches . . . who do whatever they want in resupply each time . . . and you've pictured a zoo. Los Angeles would have only one option: Carry a lifetime supply of everything.

Posting History in the Location from Whom It Should Have Come

Maybe Los Angeles can't take care of the Long Beach needs right now. They've run out of DEF 2610 and won't have any more until a week from Wednesday. Long Beach has controls based on a "reliable" supplier and a short lead time. (Remember how the Push controls are set). They've got to do something right now, so they contact the San Diego branch. "You guys show 46 DEF 2610's in stock; 2 surplus." "Could you spare us 15 total to tide us over until Los Angeles sends our normal replenishment quantity next week?" San Diego must let them have the 2 surplus, but they could say no to the other 13. Most of the time, they'll respond simply because they want help from Long Beach when they get in a bind. In comes 15 of the DEF 2610 from San Diego . . . but where is the usage posted? In Los Angeles!!

Who Do You Want to Protect for a Recurrence of the Long Beach Demand?

The usage goes in the Los Angeles record for DEF 2610. You want Los Angeles to be ready to take care of Long Beach demand the next time resupply is needed. You sure don't want San Diego to build inventory to protect for more transfers of this item to Long Beach. What just occurred was a "buddy-helping-buddy" deal . . . a *one-time* situation. Long Beach may never ask San Diego for that item again. You can see why this transfer is not posted to the San Diego usage history for DEF 2610.

On the other hand, if you don't post the usage in Los Angeles, their record for the item shows declining activity. The computer lowers the Los Angeles ordering controls on the next monthly calculation. They'll be even less able the next time to take care of Long Beach needs. Again, with many items moving back and forth between branches, the whole inventory situation spins out of control. Buyers in the warehouse revert to SWAG . . . start over-protecting to avoid getting fired . . . and you can't figure out why your magnificent central warehouse plan hasn't paid off. You have more inventory now than you had when the branches acted independently . . . and still, service to the branches stinks. The buyers guess wrong on both ends. On many items, they carry too much. For many others, not enough. SWAG nearly always has that result.

VARIATIONS ON THE CENTRAL WAREHOUSING THEME

Variations on any Central Warehouse theme can be numerous, and each requires different computer processing if resupply is to go smoothly. As mentioned earlier, there are times . . . especially on one item or a grouping . . . where the warehouse carries no stock at all to resupply branch needs. Any stock in the warehouse is for customers served from that location, but the warehouse does purchase from the outside supplier for all locations when they buy for themselves. Each branch enjoys "truckload" costs from the supplier when there's no way they could place such orders independently. In some cases, the smaller branches are not even authorized to buy direct.

The Warehouse Becomes a "Central Purchasing" Operation

The Central Warehouse buys a line of hand tools once every three weeks. This Review Cycle was developed by considering the usage per month in all locations compared to the total-order requirement of the supplier. About once every three weeks, a $5,000 order can be placed. On the night before the P.O. goes in, the computer reviews the status of every hand tool in this group in every location . . . in the warehouse and in each of the branches. A "group" purchase order goes in, combining the needs of all locations for any particular item.

Controls Used in the Branches

The branches can't use "Minimums" here . . . or at least not as they were calculated earlier in this chapter under the Push system. Instead, regular Order Points are computed for the branches with longer-than-normal lead times built-in to the calculations. Time must be allowed for the P.O. to be placed, material received back in the warehouse, and then transfer backorders filled and shipped out to all the branches. Of course if the supplier will do it, material goes to each branch directly from the supplier, rather than bringing it all into the central warehouse for redistribution. The branches also need Line Points since there's a three-week cycle between purchases. EOQ's are suitable, since each branch actually winds up being resupplied from outside the company. The purchasing step is simply being done for them. My emphasis here: Items handled like this need different controls entirely from those resupplied from warehouse stock, and the Path Code tells the computer which control-type to apply.

"Automatic" Transfer Backorders

If the Los Angeles warehouse has to accept the entire shipment from the supplier and redistribute, special programming can ease the material handling steps as well as information availability. Let's say the computer determines that the San Diego branch needs replenishment on item # STA-1010. A transfer backorder is "opened" automatically against the warehouse. It's like an open purchase order . . . except that San Diego is, in effect, placing the order against the Los Angeles warehouse. This open transfer now appears on Los Angeles' Recommended Replenishment Action Report tomorrow. The buyer in L.A. includes the San Diego requirement in his purchase. When this item is received at the warehouse from the supplier, the computer fills all backorders automatically, including the waiting transfers. While the merchandise is still in Receiving at L.A., all backorders print out. They're filled and shipped (or staged for shipment) immediately.

San Diego Can Inquire Easily about the Status

If San Diego wants to know the status of this "open order" with the L.A. warehouse, they enter the item number just as they would had it been purchased outside the company. The system shows the item on Transfer # 27004 against Los Angeles, which in turn is tied to L.A. P.O. # 70020 to the supplier. San Diego can find out the expected receipt date of this P.O. without having to call any-one at the warehouse. They're confident also that as soon as mate-rial arrives, the warehouse will fill and ship their transfer quickly. Think of the telephone calls in your company that occur today between branches and warehouse buyers trying to find out this information or to get material moving. Poor productivity . . . and as I've said in earlier chapters, time-wasting procedures like this will cripple you in the 21st century (and maybe before that).

Be Sure to Record the Transfer as "On Order"

The open transfer serves another purpose. It's initiated or opened by the computer as soon as the San Diego requirement is identi-fied. The system now shows the order quantity as "on order." That's important. Remember that the system triggers a need for replenishment when the "available for sale" stock on the shelf *plus any amount on order with the supplier,* combined, is below the Line Point at the time of this product line review. Once an "on order" quantity is recorded, the system won't try again to replenish stock on this item (unless the combination above gets low once more.)

Some systems I've seen wait until the material actually arrives in the warehouse . . . then a transfer is opened and filled. But until that happens, the branch shows nothing as "on order." On the next cycle, the computer tells the L.A. buyer to get even more for San Diego . . . when 3 months's supply, perhaps, will arrive at the warehouse tomorrow. Programming glitches like this are the reason for my gray hair. Perhaps if you heed the counsel here to watch for such programming oversights, you won't gray prematurely.

THE VARIOUS PATHS TELL THE COMPUTER
WHAT KIND OF CONTROLS TO USE

Each Replenishment Path Code tells the computer what set of controls, of which types, to use for each item in each location. The code tells the computer as well whether to open up a transfer against the warehouse or a purchase order against the supplier. It keeps you from applying the wrong control type for a particular replenishment situation. Typical replenishment path codes might look like this. These are merely suggestions. You may use, of course, any path-code scheme that works for you:

0. Item is purchased from an outside supplier. Order Point, Line Point, EOQ or Class are the controls to use.

X1. Branch 1 supplies all needs for all branches on this item . . . shipping direct to each customer. No controls are needed at the local branch. Branch 1 has records of all company usage built into their controls. Any sales order entered in any branch prints in the warehouse. The warehouse ships directly to the customer, but the selling branch receives the sales credit.

2. Item is transferred-in from Branch Number 2. Min/Max controls are used. An automatic transfer is opened against Branch 2 when the "Mininum" is reached. Computer shows the item "on order" with Branch 2 (acting as a warehouse) who ships the item automatically to the branch on the next truck.

3. Item is transferred-in from Branch Number 3, etc. Same approach as with 2. Min/Max controls are used.

20. Branch 2 buys from the supplier for you, but carries no stock of the item. Controls: Order Point, Line Point, and EOQ or Class. You must allow for a longer lead time (Branch 2 must have time to send the material on down to you after they receive it from the supplier). A Line Point is needed, since Branch 2 buys this product line on a cycle. EOQ/Class apply because you're going outside the company for this item. Do not try to apply Min/Max here.

30. Branch 3 buys from the supplier for you, just as Branch 2 did above. Same type of controls as with 20. Do not use

Min/Max. The Computer monitors your item status and alerts Branch 3 of your needs as part of their Recommended Replenishment Report for the product line just before they place the purchase order.

02. Branch 2 does carry stock, but not for you. It's for their customers. They do, however, buy their needs and your's at the same time from the outside supplier. Same type of controls apply as with 20 or 30. They'll transfer your material to you automatically as soon as they receive it. Your needs show on their RR report.

03. Branch 3 does carry stock, but not for you. Same situation except that Branch 3 does the buying. Same controls as with 02. Do not use Min/Max . . . but rather OP/LP/EOQ or Class.

D2. Branch 2 has no stock for you, places your requirements at the same time as his own with the outside supplier . . . to be shipped directly from the supplier to you. The computer in this case shows the item as "on order" with the supplier . . . not with Branch 2.

NOTE: Your system (and suppliers) should permit Branch 2 to enter the individual branch shipments as separate pages attached to a P.O. cover sheet which shows combined item quantities. P.O. number suffixes (20024-01, 20024-02, etc.) on these attachments designate material for a specific branch's shipment. These "drop-shipments" will arrive at different times with potentially different quantity or quality problems at receipt. Reconciling payment of the supplier's invoice can be a nightmare unless the entire order is entered (and invoiced) correctly.

If you have 15 branches, you could have quite a variety of path codes. Note that the last five shown here (20, 30, 02, 03, D2) reflect the "order-accumulator" function, where one location simply buys an item for any other branch who needs it at the time they're placing a normal purchase for themselves.

Agnes, Herbert . . . Somebody Must Know How to Assign These Codes

Now you see the reasons for my warnings in earlier chapters about the necessity for training as your company comes up on a system capable of this sophistication. These codes tell the computer a lot. They cause it to post usage correctly, open transfers, fill backorders automatically when shipments arrive . . . and much more. They permit a much higher level of productivity . . . information accessibility . . . reduced manual input to the computer. But the person who assigns these codes *must* understand what each does and therefore how to assign the right one to each item in a branch. This requires more training (for Agnes or Herbert or whomever you assign) in greater depth than most software packages offer. Also, the process of code-assignment is on-going. When new items are added to stock in a location, a code is assigned. Be sure that the person or people who do so have been trained as well as Agnes or Herbert were when you first installed your new system.

Resist the Urge to Shortcut the Code-Assignment Task

Furthermore, your company must *take the time* to assign these codes for each stock item as a branch begins the new system. Yes . . . someone in authority may have to ask several questions and then make a decision as to the best way for each item to be replenished. It's a tedious job. No one enjoys it. People disagree with certain path-decisions. Flexibility is taken away. The branch can no longer replenish an item any way they wish. There's also a great temptation to just "plug in" the same path on almost every item, with intent to come back later for a more-thorough decision on each one (which you likely will never do). Resist that urge. Do the job right the first time.

One More Time: Be Careful about the Software You Select!

Software that does not offer branch-control features like these will burn you badly as the 21st Century looms closer. The system may just apply EOQ's, for example, or "Min/Max" every time on every item in every branch (and the warehouse). That's all it's programmed to handle. The Inventory Management capability of the package is still mired back in the late 70's. You'll discover soon enough that it doesn't work well. You run out of stock a lot. You have huge inventories positioned in all the wrong places. The buyers and branch managers soon just dump the whole thing . . . oh, sort of silently, since the Boss bought the new package and instructed them to use it. They can't. It doesn't work in a branch network with lots of inter-branch activity. They fall back to their old comfortable SWAG, and you've gained very little from the investment in a new system.

A Correction to the 1987 Book's Advice

In "Distribution Inventory Management For The 1990's" (Pages 69 and 126–127), I offered a method of computing order points in a central warehouse which put no safety stock at all on transfers-out to other branches, when the warehouse had both sales and transfers. Safety stock was computed only on sales to customers out of the warehouse. The logic was that safety stock is already present at the branches on their sales. If it's put also on the usage-rate of transfers from the warehouse to them, then you've doubled-up. Safety has been added to the same usage twice.

Theoretically, of course, this is quite true. Realistically . . . it doesn't matter that much. My counsel now: Disregard that advice. Go ahead and put a full safety allowance on the *combination or total* of warehouse sales usage and warehouse transfers-out usage generated under proper path codes . . . in other words, when the central location acts as a true warehouse. Yes, a little extra safety stock is created. What I've found in recent years is that this isn't a serious problem . . . nor does it cause excessive inventories.

The Push Replenishment Method Requires More Safety Stock at the Warehouse

Today I feel that it's safer, and inexpensively so, to go ahead and allow more safety stock in the central warehouse . . . particularly in the light of the "Push" replenishment concept discussed earlier, where inventories in the branches are reduced and turned faster . . . but consistent and dependable resupply from the warehouse is critical. Most excess inventory isn't caused by this kind of protection. It's more often the result of "Manager Backlash," poor record accuracy, buying in the last column when that isn't justified, or SWAG ruling the replenishment decisions.

SUMMARY

Since asset mismanagement leads more distributors into bankruptcy today than any other cause, the largest asset . . . inventory . . . must be much more tightly controlled everywhere that you've made an investment in inventory. The computer's amazing capabilities now allow truly effective central control, perhaps for the first time, over these branch inventories. Branches do not "pull" stock at their own whim. Replenishment stock is "pushed" out to them as needed, to assure that their inventory dollars turn much faster than ever before. Replenishment path codes also offer programming and recording advantages to help sidestep big mistakes in inventory positioning and replenishment controls. The constant monitoring of stock conditions, placing branch requirements on reports in central locations, opening of transfers and PO's automatically, filling of backorders quickly . . . offer huge strides in personnel productivity and accuracy.

But you don't *have* to adopt any of the ideas you're reading here, of course. Your people . . . especially in Sales . . . may argue long and hard against new branch concepts, restrictions, and disciplines like these. Software that can do the things discussed here is more expensive, requiring much more training than your old system did. It's tedious and difficult to put the right information into the files as you begin. If you give in to the pressure, start pinching pennies, or get lazy, you'll almost certainly just perpetuate the same old procedures and attitudes of the past. Of course, you'll still be introduced to these new disciplines, restrictions, and these software features in the future. You'll see 'em in the company who buys you out.

Record Accuracy . . . the Foundation for Everything!

The last chapter made a big issue about the need for accurate records if you expect the "Push" warehouse/branch resupply concept to work. It mentioned "Day's-Work-In-A-Day" and Cycle Counting as prerequisites to success. Frankly, the need for this accuracy runs much deeper than that if your company expects improvement in inventory management. It undergirds *every system* related to inventory and, for that matter, productivity. What difference does it make whether you use proven ordering controls (OP, LP, EOQ, etc.) or SWAG . . . if you don't know how much of an item is out in the warehouse? Does it matter that you prefer exponential smoothing, some form of "modeling" like Focus Forecasting or my idea of the simple six-month rolling average to predict future usage . . . if only 60 of 100 stock items have accurate balances recorded in the computer? Can you expect an Inside Telephone Salesman to be truly productive with your fantastic new order entry system when he or she knows they can't trust what the system says you have available to sell . . . and must run out to the warehouse to check stock before committing anything to a customer?

Think about the Balance in Your Checkbook

Most of us are very careful to maintain an accurate balance in our checkbooks, because if we get careless . . . bad things start to happen. It would be unproductive (and financially risky) to have to call the bank each time I start to write a check: "This is ol' Graham again. How much do you show in my account *today?*" Again, all manner of plague would soon descend. So why is it that when we move over into our business mode, we permit our stock balance "accounts" to be off on 30 or more out of 100 items?

That's the accuracy rate most distributors find in the warehouse if it's been any time since the last physical inventory . . . and which items are dead on the money? You guessed it. The ones with three inventory stickers, a layer of dust, and stuff nobody wants to steal. It's the fast-moving, popular items . . . the active "accounts" that are off . . . the ones being ordered by customers and purchased from suppliers.

CYCLE COUNTING . . . REVISITED

Record accuracy, therefore, is more than a "nicety." It's *mandatory* if you expect to get the benefits of the wonderful (and expensive) new computerized system, all the in-depth training efforts, the more-professional buyers, your great new central warehouse, and software that guides toward proper replenishment action. 98 of 100 stock items must be dead accurate all the time, or within reasonable limits (+ or – 10% on washers, fasteners, o-rings, etc.). The only way to assure this day-to-day foundation for your system is to Cycle Count. The earlier book devoted an entire chapter to this, but it wasn't enough. Too many companies *still* can't seem to get an effective program going and stick with it. We need to open the subject again.

There Are Success Stories

Many distributors have put Cycle Counting to work, of course, and most are now a bit fanatical in their zeal to make sure it never fails. They'll nearly all tell you that it was the toughest accomplishment in ten years in their company. They had to fight tooth and nail to make it function properly. They'll also tell you it's made a tremendous difference in people productivity, inventory levels and profitability. Trouble is . . . only about 15% or less of the distributors in the mainline industries have succeeded. 95% could have, but they found the effort too difficult or have never even attempted a program. The reason? Management doesn't run the company. The people do.

Ask Yourself a Difficult Question

Are you willing to do a little self-analysis on your company? Would you really like to know if you can make Cycle Counting work so that you can enjoy the accurate stock balances necessary to undergird any asset management effort? OK . . . here's your question:

> How long has it been since anyone in your company has been fired for *not doing* what they were told to do?

Yes, I know you've fired people for dealing drugs, stealing, drinking, not coming to work or for being a Dallas Cowboy fan. But can you remember anyone who's been terminated for not doing as they were told? If you can't, you've sent a very clear message to all employees:

> "Be sure you come to work most of the time. Don't break any major rules. You can then do exactly what you please in the so-called disciplines of your job. We *never* fire anyone for working slowly, sloppily, lazily, carelessly, inconsistently or for not following instructions."

The Day's-Work-In-A-Day Environment

My point is this: If you're to achieve an effective cutoff in paper-flow and material movement each day . . . if you intend to crack down on who goes into the warehouse and what they do there . . . if you expect salesmen to make out the right documents when they carry out samples or make deliveries . . . all typical of the "Day's-Work-In-A-Day" working environment necessary as a prerequisite to effective Cycle Counting . . . then *YOU* have to run your company! Employees must follow directions and directives, whether they like 'em or not, whether they agree or not, whether or not it's the way they've done a job in the past. Job performance is monitored and measured, and buster, you're history if you can't or won't comply.

The "Day's-Work-In-A-Day" Checklist

It's easy to talk about working every day in a caught-up mode. Achieving such an environment is very, very difficult. However, if you'll recall the admonishment early in Chapter 1 about viewing the inventory out on your warehouse shelves as dollar bills, the need becomes obvious to remove much of the looseness most distributors have permitted in the past. Day's-Work-In-A-Day means:

1. At the close of each business day, all paperwork involving the value of the inventory in the warehouse has been processed completely. Likewise, all material is located physically where the paperwork says it should be.
2. Material is not removed from the warehouse for any reason without authorizing paperwork prepared by the proper people.
3. Again at the close of a day, the quantity found on the shelf for most stock items (exceptions discussed in a minute) is the uncommitted quantity . . . the amount still available for sale or use.

More Probing Questions

You may be thinking: "Shoot, I think we do nearly all that today." . . . but you don't. Again, ask yourself these self-analysis questions:

- Are all sales orders and transfers for stock items that are scheduled to leave the building tomorrow morning filled by the warehouse crew before they go home tonight?
- Do salesmen make deliveries but not turn in the paperwork (showing that they had material in their possession) until they return tomorrow or later?
- Are samples taken out of the building without paperwork showing who has the material?

- If you show an item as received from the supplier today, does (only) the uncommitted quantity get put up on the warehouse shelf before the crew leaves for the night?

- If you put newly-received material into stock, was the information keyed into the computer before the office staff (or whomever) went home?

- Are returns from customers put into stock before paperwork is processed giving credit to the customer or at least indicating that you now have the material back in your possession and available to sell?

- Do salesmen or order-fillers make substitutes on products of comparable value and not indicate on the paperwork that it happened?

- Do employees pull merchandise from the warehouse to make customer equipment repairs, put kits together, make conversions to basic item configurations, or do any form of assembly work . . . but not tell the system what components were used until the job is completed (kits) or billed to the customers?

- Is material moved around the warehouse to make room or to consolidate stocks . . . without telling the system of the location changes?

- Do you have a shortage procedure built-in to the credit process, whereby the units and dollars a customer says he "didn't get" are *not* automatically put back in the book value or in the available-to-sell number?

- Are there detailed procedures for handling consigned inventories either from your suppliers or to your customers? Where? How Much? Who owns? How often verified by whom? Clearly identified? How does his stock move into or back into our's?

Is All This *Really* Necessary

By now you're thinking: "Well . . . no, we don't do all that stuff, but who in the world would *want to*?" Answer: Your bank. They are very diligent to process paperwork involving dollars under their care in a complete and timely fashion every business day. They watch where their "inventory" is physically with equal dedication.

"Wait a minute, Graham! Our inventory isn't like that. It isn't negotiable currency." Hmmm . . . make that statement to your driver who just sold one of your water heaters to a dishonest customer on his route at 100% gross margin (to the driver). He turned that water heater into cash as quick as a wink . . . faster even than he can cash his pay check.

Make your grand pronouncement to the Controller next January when the company must write off a $168,000 shortage in the Des Moines branch after the year-end inventory. It wasn't theft in Des Moines . . . just sloppiness in many of the areas above all through the year. Say it to the next customer who's mad as a wet hen when you can't deliver merchandise (dollars) you showed to have. He decides to order any further dollars from your competitor.

Distributors Need a Banking Lesson

Remember the Number 1 cause of bankruptcy today in distribution: Mismanaged assets. Not lack of sales. Not underpaid executives. Not overstaffed operations. The Number 1 asset of most distributors is inventory. Most of the inventory they own is in their warehouse(s). All manner of paperwork affecting the value of this asset flies around the company like confetti raining down on a parade . . . some under control . . . some with little control . . . some with none at all. It's not that way at the bank.

Does the bank do a "Day's-Work-In-A-Day"? You'd better believe it. Do they get more deposits, for example, on the 1st and the 15th than any other time? Do they process *all* deposits . . . no matter how many . . . by the time they go home if received prior to the close of banking hours? Of course. What would happen if they didn't? My checks would bounce. The bank replies:

> "Hey, Graham, I know you're upset about your checks not being covered . . . but be reasonable. You made your deposit last Friday, the 1st, when we were buried by people coming in here. We'll get to your deposit by Wednesday sure. Just hold off on your checks until then."

Or what if the armored car makes a late delivery of cash? Gosh, and with the Labor Day weekend coming up too . . . so the bank employees manage to get the stuff inside the lobby and sign the "packing slip." Then they take off for the lake. They'll put the inventory away properly next Tuesday (if enough vault employees show up after the holiday). The office staff noticed a big pile of checks that arrived this morning and they're supposed to get all those posted off the various accounts . . . but heck, two employees need to go by the cleaners on the way home, and another is leaving on vacation. They just blow off those checks. "They'll be waiting next Tuesday," a wise prophet says. Sounds pretty stupid doesn't it? Yet, that's just the way many distributors treat their "cash" (in another form) or paperwork involving their "cash."

More Silliness

How about samples? Wouldn't it be nice if people from the bank's Sales Department would drop by my office to say:

> "Sir, here are a few 20's of the type we'll pay you if you'll keep your money in our bank. Why don't you use these and see if they're helpful. If you decide to give us your business, we'll pay you even more of these."

Sounds like the way some of the Savings & Loans operated in the past, doesn't it? But if this practice becomes popular, my point is this: The guy who checks out the "samples" would be required to have proper paperwork. The bank wouldn't let their inventory out the door in an employee's possession with no paperwork just because he has a 20-year pin. They probably wouldn't let him come into the place after hours on a Saturday night, take some "stock" and make a delivery to a customer who had an emergency need for cash . . . not without a vault employee to check him in and out and be sure the withdrawal paperwork was in order. Are you getting the message? You, too, are dealing with *DOLLARS!!* Stop treating them like they're something else.

A bank treats the money as money. It's safeguarded. Paperwork involving its value is processed carefully and completely. Very accurate records are kept on *all* accounts . . . not just 70%. Yes, there are "cutoffs," to assure that there's time to get all assigned work done before the employees go home. Distributors must adopt a similar attitude or the 21st century will be a nightmare. Certainly the problems are more difficult, because the inventory takes many shapes and sizes, but the objective is the same as the bank's.

SPECIAL PROGRAMMING HELPS THE OVERALL OBJECTIVE

Cycle Counting must become a way of life, and yes, it too is very difficult to implement successfully. Every tool available has to help out, and the most powerful tool we have is the computer. New programming is needed in some sticky areas involving "Day's-Work-In-A-Day." You should develop capabilities to identify Level 1 and Level 2 Commitments, and "Future" sales orders require a set of unique steps as well.

Level 1 Commitments

Visualize this scene:

Right now on one of our popular stock items, we have 100 on hand out in the warehouse, and none of the 100 has been committed to anyone. The available-for-sale balance is also 100.

A customer calls: "I want 20 of this item delivered out to me on your truck tomorrow morning." As soon as this sales order is keyed into the computer, the records now look like this:

On Hand	Level 1 Commitment	Available To-Sell Balance
100	20	80

Since this order is for delivery tomorrow, it becomes a "Level 1" Commitment. A picking ticket prints in the warehouse, and the available-for-sale balance is reduced to 80 units immediately. Only 80 are now available to any other customer or salesman who calls in five minutes later.

The warehouse crew must fill the order before they can go home tonight. They don't have to ship the order . . . just fill and "stage" it for shipment tomorrow morning. The Shelf Count for this item, when the lights are turned off this evening, will be 80. Note that the Shelf Count and Available-for-Sale balance are the same at day's end. Here's the picture in the computer records:

On Hand	Level 1 Commitment	Shelf Count	Available To-Sell Balance
100	20	80	80

Level 2 Commitments

However, this company location also serves as a central warehouse for branch needs, in addition to selling to local area customers. Harry in the branch 50 miles away calls: "On next Wednesday's truck, I need 30 of this item for my stock." Now the picture looks like this:

On Hand	Level 1 Commitment	Shelf Count	Level 2 Commitment	Available To-Sell Balance
100	20	80	30	50

Harry's need for stock is almost a week away. It's a "Level 2" Commitment. Certainly the Available-To-Sell balance must be reduced as soon as the transfer is keyed into the system. We don't want another salesman to double-commit the stock should an order be received late this afternoon.

But it isn't necessary for the warehouse crew to fill the transfer until next Tuesday evening. The Shelf Count we'd expect to find on this item tonight when all activity ceases is 80. They have to fill and stage tonight only the Level 1 commitments. In fact, only Level 1 orders are printed in the warehouse. Level 2 commitments are not printed . . . until they change status and move into Level 1 (next Tuesday night for the transfer to go to Harry's branch on Wednesday's truck).

Warehouse Discipline Must Be Enforced

Strict warehouse discipline is mandatory. If we do take another sales order late today for 60 units, a picking ticket goes to the warehouse with these numbers: "Ship 50. Backorder 10." But when the warehouseman walks up to the shelf, how many does he find there? Right . . . 80.

What might happen? He goes ahead and fills the full 60 on his new order, figuring that the computer is fouled up. If that happens, we'll break both his legs very slowly . . . one at a time.

From that point forward, Mr. Warehouse Manager, you must fill and stage *every* commitment of any type . . . Level 1 or 2 . . . before your crew goes home each night.

"We don't have enough room to do that !!" . . . he protests. OK, then *do exactly what we tell you to do on every order. Never take material from the shelf unless we authorize it on the picking ticket.*

The Level 1 and Level 2 Commitments Make Cycle Counting More Workable

It's rather obvious that every commitment against available stock need not be pulled from the shelf each night before the warehouse crew leaves. Yet . . . Cycle Counting, if effective, requires a solid "Day's-Work-In-A-Day" environment. By developing and enforcing a "Shelf Count" for some items, a counter may still verify the accuracy and make corrections to the computer records, even when all commitments have not been pulled physically from the shelves (as advised in my earlier book). For example, let's say that our counter tonight finds only 78 on the shelf for the item we've been working with:

On Hand	Level 1 Commitment	Expected Shelf Count	Level 2 Commitment	Available To-Sell Balance
100	20	80	30	50
		78		
−2	← Adjustment To On Hand	Actual Count	Adjustment To Available →	−2

Making Adjustments to the Records and in Accounting

Adjustments of minus 2 units are made in both directions. In addition to dropping the shelf count by 2 pieces, the "On Hand" comes down 2 and the "Available-to-Sell balance also is reduced by

2. The inventory dollar-value that seems to have disappeared is placed in a special "holding account." Next week, a count on some other row of the warehouse may uncover an offsetting dollar value on the high side. The holding account gets both pluses and minuses added all through the year. At year-end, it should have washed out. If it doesn't . . . then a book inventory adjustment should be made.

The key point here is that it's unreasonable to expect the warehouse to fill and stage commitments that lie too far into the future. The Level 2 and Shelf Count programming solves that problem to allow effective Cycle Counting.

FUTURE ORDERS

Programming feature Number 2, needed to assist a Cycle Count effort, involves "future" sales orders. Here's the scene:

> One of our best customers sends in an order for 70 pieces of a popular stock item. He needs delivery August 1st, but today is April 20th. Now what? If we put this requirement into the system . . . even as a Level 2 commitment . . . it drops the Available-to-Sell balance. That balance triggers the Line and Order Points, so we could wind up reordering stock far too early.

> On the other hand, why is he giving us the order now? Because he wants to make *absolutely certain* we provide the stock on August 1st. His need is critical to meet that date.

Good programming solves the dilemma. The sales order is given a special order-handling code . . . as a "Future." The computer checks the average lead time from our supplier for the item the customer wants. It's 3 weeks. It then backs off the August 1st date by 3 weeks, plus another week for safety, and specifies July 1st as the date for this sales order to be put into the Level 2 Commitment category.

On July 1st, the Available-to-Sell balance is reduced. If we don't have enough stock to take care of the August 1st order, there's time to place a new purchase order with the supplier. If we wait to check this within the 3-week lead time window and find we're low on stock . . . we're dead. But it's too costly to commit the stock now on April 20th and almost certainly bring in more inventory from the supplier long before it's really needed.

Insist on These Software Features

Aren't you glad you have a computer system that handles problems like this smoothly? Oh you don't. Well, when you pick your next package, be sure it has features like the Level 1 and Level 2 Commitments, developing a Shelf Count, and special handling of Future orders. They'll save you some grief, but more importantly . . . they make Cycle Counting easier to implement.

CYCLE COUNTING VERSUS THE QUARTERLY PHYSICAL

Occasionally, a distributor in one of my training sessions argues:

> "Look Gordon, you say to count each item four times a year in a Cycle Counting program . . . but wouldn't I achieve the same results with four full inventories a year, one each quarter? Instead of having counters out in the warehouse every night, I'll just bring in the full crew four times a year on a Saturday. It seems much easier . . . many less problems."

That approach gets some of the benefits of a full Cycle Count effort, but it misses one of the most important advantages. The primary objective of "Day's-Work-In-A-Day" is to run the company in a "caught-up" state every day, with all paperwork processed and all material positioned properly and completely when employees take off every afternoon. This prerequisite is necessary, remember, if Cycle Counting is to be effective. But "Day's-Work-In-A-Day" brings with it another huge (but hidden to a degree) advantage.

Improved Productivity

Just imagine the nasty problems you'll face tomorrow and the fires that'll have to be put out . . . *because you don't* work in such a caught-up mode right now in your company. Think of the many manhours of unproductive effort expended to find information or run down the source of a problem that would've been unnecessary if " . . . everything had been posted." Visualize the time warehouse people will spend looking for material or trying to find misplaced paperwork. Think of the customers who'll be given incorrect or incomplete information, and the countless steps that have to be done over to correct the mistakes that result. Consider the lost sales when you don't have up-to-date balances for material in other branch locations . . . that might have been offered in place of an item you don't have at the moment locally. Count how many times one of your employees relies on the "Problem Solving Flowchart" (page 102) when something goes wrong . . . the "CYA" (Cover Your Assets) mode. Expensive !

Employees Learn Quickly

When you elect to take just four inventories a year, rather than a little piece of the inventory 200 evenings during the year, the employees learn a very critical fact:

"You really have to get caught-up around here just four times a year. Yes, on that Friday before we count each quarter, you'd better work like crazy. The rest of the time, it's business as usual. Nobody breaks a sweat. Paperwork lags along for processing whenever we get around to it, and material is handled in our time-honored manner: If it ain't in the way, let it lay!"

With Day's-Work-In-A-Day, you have to be caught-up *all the time on all items and all paperwork* . . . because you don't know precisely which areas or items will be counted tonight. Unless you've worked in this mode, you likely cannot even imagine how much smoother you can function or the increased productivity with personnel. This one benefit: Being caught-up *every* day . . . is worth all the

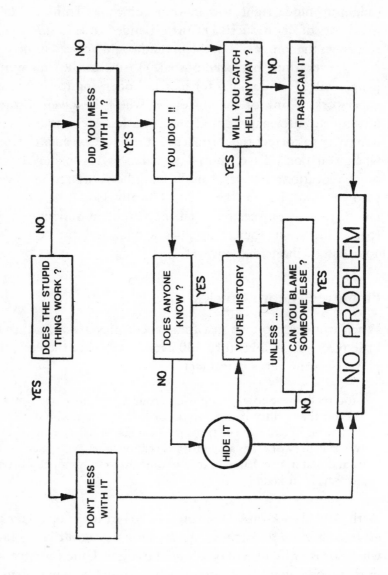

PROBLEM SOLVING FLOWCHART

grief, gnashing of teeth, gray hair and Rolaids you'll see as you try to implement a program in your company.

THEFT . . . MORE OF A PROBLEM THAN YOU REALIZE

Finally in this chapter, let's discuss some ugly statistics:

- 20% of your employees will never steal from you.
- 20% will steal, regardless of what you do to prevent it.
- 60% are not thieves, generally, but if you make it easy enough and they need the money bad enough . . . they too will steal.

Scary, isn't it? 8 out of 10 employees will steal often or occasionally. If you fail to recognize this . . . and do nothing about it . . . you can forget record accuracy. Maybe any hope of profits as well. Management's job is to make it **very difficult** to steal and crack down hard when it happens.

The Undercover Detective

You might begin by hiring an undercover detective to work for you out in the warehouse as a regular employee. It's expensive. This guy or gal may come at $30–40 per hour, plus normal pay for warehouse work. They may have to be out there for 90 days or more before they uncover all that's going on. However, their day doesn't end at 5 PM. They go bowling with the other employees, go on fishing trips, and attend the Yankees game with the crew. They work their way into the confidence and inner circle of the warehouse employees. If you have any drug users or dealers, they'll identify them. If you have any thieves or (worse) theft rings operating, they'll find out who, when and how. For many situations, this is the only way you'll uncover these activities before they cripple profits.

Avoid Prosecution if You Can

When you catch your thief (not if . . . **WHEN**), my suggestion is to have the police show up and make quite a spectacle of the arrest. Parade him through the warehouse in custody and into your office. Everyone in the place sees it happen. Here's what you say to him:

> "Tommy, we've got the goods on you. You've been stealing for a long time. You're history around here. Get out of here and don't ever come back. We're not going to file charges against you . . . unless you file for unemployment compensation or some kind of labor suit against us. If you do either of those, we'll then take you to court, produce our evidence, and do all we can to put you away for several years."

Tommy knows he's been stealing. He won't contest getting fired, and he's very relieved that he won't get an extended vacation at government expense. He won't risk making too big a stink, for fear that you will indeed produce evidence (exactly what . . . he doesn't know) that convicts him. Likely, he'll disappear and you won't hear of him again. No labor suit. No unemployment compensation claim. One less thief on the payroll.

Why Not Prosecute?

If you do take Tommy to court, your undercover detective must appear and testify. Now everybody in your company will know how you caught ol' Tommy. I want them to know *that* we caught him . . . that he was *fired for stealing,* but not *how* this was done. In a week or so, my detective will quit the company. I intend to use that technique again in the future from time to time, to see what's going on in the warehouse. However, if the employees out there knew how we caught Tommy . . . they won't trust any new employees for 12 years. You can never effectively use that approach again. Besides, I just want to be rid of Tommy . . . not brand him for life. Since 60% of the employees steal only on occasion, we'll give Tommy a break. Maybe this experience will scare him enough to keep him from doing it again. And we can also use the detective-approach again.

Ride with Deliverymen Once in a While

If you make deliveries on your own trucks, Mr. Branch Manager, then ever so often just go out in the morning, climb on board with a driver, and announce that you're going to ride with him today. The excuse: "I'm going to take a little informal survey today on how the customers like our delivery service!." The real reason: To see if any merchandise is on that truck at day's end for which there's no official paperwork. If you find unauthorized stock on the truck at the end of the run, schedule a long talk with both driver and loader.

A common theft tactic is for one "inside" employee to work with an "outside" partner. The guy who loaded that truck last night or this morning, and who's supposed to check on the material, has formed a business with the driver. Whatever the driver sells the extra stuff for (even 10 cents on the dollar) is 100% profit to these two. You now have a silent partnership helping you with inventory turns.

Don't Let "Paperwork Theft" Burn You

One distributor told me that of his ten branch managers, eight were stealing through a sloppy paperwork system. The managers had discovered that the company would pay any invoice from any supplier if they approved it. Each had gone to a printer and had official-looking invoices prepared for fictitious companies. They'd then mail themselves an invoice from, let's say, "ABC Industries" with a post office box reply-address. They'd approve the invoice, mail it to corporate . . . who'd set up a new supplier in the file, cut a check, and mail it to the P.O. box. The manager would get the check, endorse it as "ABC Industries," and deposit it in an ABC Industries checking account . . . on which he wrote the checks. His name never appeared on the check anywhere. A vast sum had been stolen that way.

The company had omitted a simple, yet critical step anytime a new supplier is requested for the file. Call the telephone number given. See who answers. Run a credit check on the company. Insist on talking to other customers. Just make sure it's a real company . . . not a dummy being used to siphon off money.

SUMMARY

Distributors need a fresh, new attitude about running a business. Historically, we've plugged along in a sloppy, informal, undisciplined, laid-back manner with a "Scarlett O'Hara" mindset: "Hey, if it's tough or troublesome . . . we'll worry about that tomorrow!" Sorry. We have to worry about it *today!* The inventory represents big stacks of dollar bills in another form, and every scrap of paper . . . every piece of stock . . . involving that inventory must be processed or handled properly every day. We must use tough methods to guard against or deal with theft . . . just as a bank does. The records for our "dollars" must be 98% accurate all the time. Our system depends on it. Our productivity levels are enhanced or crippled by it. It's not overly-dramatic to say that our survival in the 21st century may very well be tied to it.

Pay Scales and
Performance Standards 8

This chapter won't be as long as some of the others. The exhortation, though important, need not be long-winded for two reasons:

(1) You're not going to like the advice at all.
(2) You'll need time for medical attention or counseling after reading it.

In fact, if you're the Boss in your company, you'd do well to go ahead now and take a Valium . . . or something to tranquilize you. If you have blood pressure problems, have a nurse standing by as you read on. I'm about to suggest that you invest more money than you have in the past in another critical asset of your company . . . the people.

Pay Scales of the Past Reveal More Than You Realize

Although never stated openly, many distributors in the past gave away their true attitudes about relative job importance by their pay scales:

> "Let's be sure that we function with highly-paid, well-motivated, (sometimes) highly-skilled, excellent system-supported salesmen in the field . . . but back them up with low-pay, poorly-motivated, low-skill, poorly system-supported people in the warehouse and in Purchasing."

Employees coming to work in these companies learned quickly where they could earn the best pay . . . Sales! Any other assignment was looked on as an "apprenticeship." Do whatever you have to do to move on out of that area as fast as possible, and get assigned to the Counter, to Inside Sales, and finally to Outside Sales. The best employees never remained in the warehouse or in Purchasing very long. If someone did, he or she was viewed as "unfit for a sales position," or perhaps they had no real ambition or drive. You can imagine the costly imbalance this caused in the operation.

A Lesson from Football

In the last chapter, the banking business offered a much-needed lesson for distributors. As we move into the sensitive area of pay scales, professional football provides a good model. For example, what if the Dallas Cowboys followed the distributors' old line of logic?

> "Gosh, player salaries are becoming a major expense. From here on, we'll pay only the offensive team players an average of $600,000 each per year. Defensive people will be hired at minimum wage. They hardly ever score touchdowns anyway . . . and let's petition the league for a rules change so that we have to play only nine players on defense. That ought to reduce our salary expense."

If they followed through on something dumb like this, what results could they expect? . . . hmmm, about what they had in the 80's and early 90's, but that wasn't their intent or plan. The defensive players are paid big money. Interestingly, they aren't really expected to score touchdowns. If they happen to get one . . . great . . . but that's simply a by-product of their primary purpose: *To Support The Offense!* How do they do that? By getting the ball back without letting the other team's offense score. And often, the best athletes are put on defense.

Dallas can't afford to put an underpaid defensive unit out there, or try to get by with only nine guys when the other team fields eleven. Underpayment would mean that they couldn't sign their draft picks, and they'd have to suit up people who'd be willing to play for the low salaries. With only nine on the defensive unit, just a few snaps would decide the game's outcome.

Why Do Distributors Permit the Imbalance?

This ridiculous analogy leads to a basic question: "If doing something stupid like that in football would lead to a last-place finish and no fans, then why do distributors try to compete with such an imbalanced team?" The answer is found again in our history. Most distributors are still sales "dominated" . . . not sales "oriented."

The owner or President remembers what "built the business" back in the 60's or 70's. The company started small, of course, and in those early days survival depended on the next sale. Sales were the life-blood of the company, and most of the effort, worry, planning, staff development, nurturing, and lost sleep revolved around sales. All other activities were secondary. Each had to get along the best it could . . . with the people and/or budget that could be spared. The best people had to be assigned to sales, and they had to be retained . . . so any funds available for compensation were again focused in the primary area of concern. The company survived because times were generally good . . . an inflationary economy, cheap money, equally inept competition, and there was plenty of business to go around in most years.

The Times Changed . . . Distributors Didn't

We've been over this ground before, but when the economic climate and business conditions changed (for good) in the early 80's . . . many distributors kept right on the same old path. They didn't recognize the new requirement for asset management. The stayed with the same formula of earlier years, even when the company's assets were now far greater . . . far more widespread . . . far more decentralized and out from under the watchful eye of the owner.

The 80's move on into the 90's. Interest rates climb, inflation slows, recessions begin to occur much more frequently, and still . . . there are no professionals on board other than in Sales and maybe now, Accounting. Better computer systems evolve as well, and competitors begin to make use of them . . . but again, many distributors keep the blinders on: They maintain a sales "dominated" posture. Good ol' Charlie continues to buy under the same SWAG of years past, and Agnes (now 68 years old) is his helper . . . but instead of buying only $500,000 annually as in 1975 . . . this pair now spends $6 million per year.

"Graham, Get to the Point!"

How do you change this stance to one that's sales "oriented"? Begin by beefing up the support areas of the company . . . specifically Purchasing and Warehousing. OK, now pop that Valium. Here it comes:

> You should start entry-level Purchasing assistants or buyers at $30,000 per year. With experience, a Buyer should expect to earn between $50,000 and $70,000 annually . . . *AND* a Buyer is assigned no more than 5,000 stock items to control, and all non-stock items of course that are related.

"You're nutso, Graham. When Charlie retired, we raised Agnes to $1,500 a month and she handles all 17,000 stock items. It's worked out fine." Yes, it's true: Agnes doesn't seem to work all that hard. She often leaves each day at 5:00.03 P.M. The Salesmen are quite pleased with her performance. Service is excellent. However, when you try to push the warehouse doors open, they seem obstructed. Finally, you're able to squeeze on through and you discover what's blocked the doors . . . *a massive inventory!* That's the only way Agnes can do the job. She's buried by 17,000 items. There's no time for a professional approach that would provide good service but keep the inventory down. She just keeps a lifetime supply of everything out there. . . and at her salary, if you really pressed her to perform better, she'd walk out. Her replacement would be an untrained "Agnes," and you'd **really** be in the soup.

What's Your Attitude about Sales Territory Coverage?

To see the misguided thinking, ask yourself this question: "If a key salesman quit tomorrow, how long would you permit his critical sales territory to be left unassigned . . . or perhaps handled by doubling-up the workload of another salesman?" "Not long at all," you reply. "We must be sure that all major customers are called-on regularly, and an overworked salesman would let something important slip through the crack." Nothing wrong with your logic there. It makes perfect sense . . . and yet in a major support function, you've given Agnes 17,000 items to buy, and she's paid whatever she'll work for. She also spends millions of your dollars each year using warmed-over SWAG (learned from her mentor, Charlie). What's the Number 1 reason for distributor bankruptcy? Uncovered sales territories? Overworked salesmen? Hmmm . . . no, as I recall, it's something else: *TOO MUCH INVENTORY . . . MISMANAGED ASSETS!* Aren't your assets worth the organizational structure to be sure that buyers are not overloaded? Aren't they worth a payroll investment that insures you can have professionals assigned to the management task?

THE WAREHOUSE

There's a similar problem in the warehouse for many distributors. Here too, you may be trying to get by with low-pay, low-skill labor. Of course, the crew out there changes constantly. Nobody stays very long, and the ones who do are generally incompetent. Dead lice wouldn't fall off of one of your warehousemen, because they move at a very leisurely pace. If you attempted to crack down, the whole bunch would walk out. They can get just as good a job as this one in 50 places around town. Not only that . . . they're stealing you blind, and if you could legally give them a polygraph, shoot, they'd pass it. The way they see it, they're not stealing at all. They're just working out their own private "compensation programs."

Somebody Has to "Compensate" for Them

With such laggards taking care of the critical warehouse functions
. . . receiving, putting material away, moving it, counting it, order-
filling, and shipping . . . disaster is commonplace. Material is
shipped wrong. It's received wrong. It's put in the wrong place.
Salesmen have to go in the warehouse all the time to fill their own
orders or double-check what was done. The computer records stink,
of course, because "Day's-Work-In-A-Day" with this warehouse
crew is only a dream and Cycle Counting unworkable. Salesmen are
out there all the time checking stock, getting their own samples,
breaking into kits, seeing what's in Receiving, and often making
their own deliveries.

While salesmen are doing all these little tasks (some necessary
and some that just cause more trouble), what are they *NOT* doing?
Yeah . . . they're not selling! But what can you say? They *have to*
go out there. They certainly can't trust the warehouse people to do
anything right. The salesmen are the offensive team. They score the
touchdowns, but they're getting lousy support from the defense
. . . so they have to play both ways. Something slips through the
crack now for sure.

Stand by for a Heart-Massage

You should start your warehouse people at $12 to $15 per hour.
OK, go ahead and call 911 for the coronary unit. I *know* your heart
is now beating out of rhythm. Your pulse is triple what it was a
minute ago. "Graham, you're going to bankrupt us with these pay
scales!," you scream. The truth is . . . they won't. Instead, they'll
attract the warehousing professionals from your area over to your
company. The benefits:

A. They won't leave. They can't get a job as good as this one
   anywhere else in town.

B. They'll do exactly what you tell them to, and they come to
   work dependably. They don't want to lose this job.

C. They won't (as a rule) steal from you, for the same reason and
   the fact that they're paid well enough to live. They don't
   need to steal.

D. They'll show up the performance of older employees, who may now demonstrate clearly that they cannot meet your new work standards. You can get rid of the laggards and, for this money, attract more professionals.

E. One of these pros is worth four of the type warehousemen you have now. It doesn't require as many of them to get the work completed.

One distributor who's followed this approach went a step further. He had business cards printed for each warehouse employee, with the title: "Assistant Warehouse Manager." Why not? When you think about it, that's precisely what each productive warehouseman really is. The people have pride in their jobs and their contribution to the company's success.

Low Pay Breeds a Consistent Level of (Non) Performance

At your current warehouse pay, if you somehow hire a real go-getter out there, he'll work only a short while before one of the other employees corners him or her and says:

"Listen Jack (or Jacqueline), you're making us all look bad. If you want to drive home on inflated tires tonight, you'd better slow down about four notches."

Of course, the professional quits the next day. He or she simply refuses to work in an environment where you can't get ahead with hard, intelligent effort. "Why can't we ever keep a good warehouseman?," you ask. Now you know.

Cycle Counting and "Day's-Work-In-A-Day" Require Good People

The last chapter went on and on about record accuracy, doing all the work each day that the day brings, and maintaining a caught-up mode. Just *try* it with some of your current warehouse employees. "They don't pay me enough around here to work **that** hard! They

can blow off that program . . . and if they press me, I'm history."
. . . and what do you get for a replacement? An untrained ware-house guy with the same attitude.

To make Cycle Counting pay off, you must be able to depend on warehouse people who follow directions and work smart . . . even when nobody's around to check up on 'em. It's never going to work perfectly, and there'll always be a few who won't perform regard-less of the pay. But there's no chance of success with a universal attitude problem in the warehouse brought on by low pay that in turn breeds employees who couldn't care less about any aspect of the job.

REMEMBER FEDERAL EXPRESS

I'm told that when Federal Express first moved into Memphis, they followed the concept recommended here . . . and paid higher scales than anyone in the area had ever seen for the type work they expected. The critics jumped them: "Boy, you won't make it paying that kind of money around here!" What happened? Federal Express attracted the cream of the work force in Memphis to their opera-tion. They stayed. They learned. They improved. They worked like beavers to keep these great jobs. Productivity-per-employee was (and still is) outstanding. Poor Federal Express. I hope they make it.

How to Get Started

Why not call the entire warehouse crew together one afternoon and tell them:

"Effective Monday, everyone out here will get a $3 hour raise."

Let the cheering die down. Sidestep the big container of Gatoraid they'll try to pour on you. Then continue:

"Now also effective Monday, this is the way things are going to be done out here. Here are the standards of performance for each of your jobs. We will see quickly which of you can raise your performance to these levels and which can't hack it. If you can't or won't come up to these levels . . . you'll be terminated. For this money, we'll find people who want to do the job as it must be done from here on."

Surprisingly, some of the current crew will rev up several RPM's and perform better than you ever dreamed they could. Others can't . . . or won't. Get rid of that bunch. For this warehouse pay, you'll now attract the cream of the warehousing professionals from your area. Sure, careful screening is required and there'll be a few trial-and-error missteps, but you'll sift down to the best crew you've ever had . . . and likely with not as many as before. Now you've got pro's to support pro's, and the salesmen are to stay out of the warehouse. "Offense . . . tend to your business! The Defense will now support you beautifully."

"What If We Have a Union?"

Dealing with a union is more difficult, of course, but you can still make major strides. When the contract is next due for renegotiation, tell the union representatives:

> "The company has decided to raise each warehouse employee's pay by $3 per hour in the new contract. You may carry that news immediately to your membership. What we will now negotiate is precisely what each job requires . . . the standards of job performance, how an employee is measured, terminated, etc. If you battle us too hard on these points, we will re-open the pay issue."

Increased pay and/or benefits are always seen by union members as "victory" in a new contract. For such healthy increases, they know that the other shoe's got to fall somewhere in all this. They *want* that increased pay. The negotiators are put in a solid position also. Hey, they'll be viewed as hero's. They need not explain that the company made the pay offer up-front without any haggling from them. To get it, all they had to agree to was a new set of performance standards, measurements and termination procedures. True, these are important conciliations ". . . but goodnight members, we had to give in on something to get *this* kind of pay increase!"

SUMMARY

Pay scales reveal the true picture as to how the various jobs in your company are ranked by Management. No matter what you say, how you *pay* uncovers your real priorities quite clearly to every employee . . . especially new ones. The compensation possible in Job A versus Job B, for about the same amount of effort and brainpower, cause the good employees to move rapidly into the better-paying jobs. Other functions are then relegated to people not as smart, not as skilled, and those just putting in 8 hours and who have no ambition for anything better.

The support functions . . . those that support your sales effort and the salespeople . . . must be staffed by professionals. The most obvious support activities are Purchasing and Warehousing. Historically, distributors often took the "poor-boy" approach in one or both of these, while giving rather obvious emphasis to Sales functions through the pay scales. No one argues the importance of the sales force or that they should be paid very well, but the pay imbalance must be corrected as you move on out of the 90's and into the 21st century.

The Dallas Cowboys don't want to lose a game by the score of 48 to 112. The "defense" is just as important to winning as the "offense." Be sure that you draft some Number 1 picks for *your* support functions, and then follow up by paying the money necessary to keep them from becoming free agents.

The Economic Order Quantity (EOQ) . . . Revisited

9

OK. The first eight chapters have badgered you about all manner of topics related to computers, Inventory Management, branches and a more profitable, productive operation. Those are all important with any system of ordering controls you apply to replace Agnes' or Charlie's SWAG. But the controls themselves have to be understood completely and implemented where they fit, or again . . . the results will be unsatisfactory. You'll be unhappy with your computerized system, the software house, your buyers, or all of the above. The Boss will be unhappy with you. Your future will become cloudy. You may have to try consulting . . . and since I don't want you out here competing with me, you'd better pay close attention to these next chapters. In this one, we'll discuss the order quantity.

"Grahamology" Is Gaining Wider Acceptance

As the years move along, more distributors are becoming aware of the concepts I've been preaching . . . things like Order Points, Line Points and EOQ's. Distributors seem to like the controls because they apply common sense and simple mathematics in helping a buyer to answer difficult questions: When and how much to buy of a stock item? The controls offer understandable options to

SWAG. They produce predictable results. Most distributors would prefer, however, not to have to program these controls themselves . . . which would mean they'd have to go through all the learning curves and missteps required to build the system from scratch on a computer. Instead, they look around for some outfit who's already done it to sell them software or a complete hardware/software package. The software companies have climbed on board as well . . . or at least a number of them have. With a growing market for software that includes these concepts, more packages surface each year which claim to have incorporated the Graham controls and philosophy.

A CLEAR INDICATION OF POOR SOFTWARE

Some software outfits comply but only superficially. They buy a copy of "Distribution Inventory Management For The 1990's," read it quickly, and draw an immediate conclusion:

> "Hmmm . . . this guy Graham talks a lot about EOQ's and gives a programmable formula. So *that's* what our prospects are asking for! They want to use EOQ's."

The programming staff adds EOQ's to the system capabilities. When a prospect says that they want a package following Graham's concepts, the salesman replies:

> "No problem. Look at this screen here. See the 'EOQ' field. Just say you want to use EOQ's in the system set-up parameters, and our package calculates them for every item as the suggested quantity to buy. We built our system around Graham's book."

EOQ and "Order Quantity" Are *NOT* Synonymous

The systems house has made a grave error: They've assumed that EOQ . . . the Economic Order Quantity formula . . . is synonymous with replenishment order quantity. You certainly do *not* use EOQ's every time, on every item, in every branch, in every condition. It's a wonderful tool to help guide the order quantity decision in stock replenishment, but like any tool, it works in some applications and not in others. Any software package that applies EOQ blindly across the board . . . or makes it easy for the user to do so . . . should be avoided like the plague. You'll get into big trouble with that package.

When Is EOQ Used? When Is It the Wrong Tool?

EOQ serves well as the proper order quantity control in these conditions:

1. There's no quantity price break offered by the supplier for this one individual item.
2. The source of resupply is outside the company . . . not from another branch.
3. The item is not seasonal.
4. Usage per month is at least $1/2$ unit . . . six per year.
5. The item is not being purchased under a blanket order with scheduled release dates.

These five conditions . . . when present . . . call for some other method of developing the replenishment order quantity. EOQ is

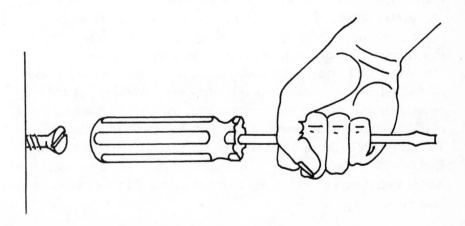

out of it's element. It doesn't, for example, consider the possibility of a better cost from the supplier when a larger quantity of the single item is ordered. That situation requires a computerized evaluation of the discount schedule to see how far up you can go before savings are offset by holding costs.

When resupply is from another company location, central warehouse or branch, remember that "Min/Max" is more likely the better control approach. On seasonal items, as you read in an earlier chapter, the system should recommend a purchase that covers the next three months of anticipated usage only. When usage is low, arbitrary controls are set manually. Blanket order release quantities also are determined by logic outside of EOQ's realm.

EOQ IS MATHEMATICAL . . . IT DOESN'T APPLY COMMON SENSE, SO YOU MUST

Even when EOQ is applicable, the formula can still yield strange answers if attempted with "fringe-area" items. From the earlier book's discussion of the EOQ formula, recall that it balances out the incremental cost of holding an item in stock with the cost of going through a replenishment cycle. In doing this, EOQ develops a purchase quantity that assures the lowest possible "outgoing" cost . . . the lowest accumulation of all costs . . . for the average unit of stock as it goes out the door to a customer.

Remember also that a $5 Replenishment-Cycle Cost for most products is suggested along with a carrying cost in the 30% per year range (although they're not always these values, as we'll see later in this chapter). When a stock item has a very low unit cost and also low usage, EOQ may tell you buy 10 year's supply. It would take that long before the incremental holding cost would offset the $5 order-cycle expense. Example: An o-ring selling 5 per month and costing a penny. Conversely, if the item has a very high unit cost and also high usage (a $600 compressor that sells 50 per month), EOQ may advise you to buy 10 minutes's supply. The $5 cycle cost is offset very, very quickly when so much money moves through the inventory.

COMPUTERIZED "FENCES" PROTECT YOU FROM THE NON-THINKING FORMULA

You may be getting the idea that EOQ is too dangerous to use. Please don't. EOQ is an *excellent* way to set replenishment order quantities on many stock items. It does a beautiful job . . . most of the time. A power saw needs a guard for safety. The arc-welder wears dark glasses to protect his eyes. Many effective tools require some form of "protection" if they're to be used without injury. EOQ is a tool also. It needs "fences" built around the answers to keep it from harming you. Program these boundaries around *any* order quantity formula or check out prospective software to be sure the designers considered them:

1. Round the formula's answer to the *nearest* standard pack or pallet quantity. This standard pack quantity comes from the master inventory record for the item.

2. The answer may *never* be more than 1 year's supply. The computer simply cuts back to the usage rate times 12, and then rounds off to standard pack.

3. Only rarely should the answer represent less than two weeks' supply. We can't say "never" here, because there are conditions where you do bring in less (an extremely high-volume item where two truckloads arrive weekly, etc.) but these are rare. "Flow Points" to control such items are discussed in Chapter 10.

4. Make certain the calculated order quantity represents at least the Review Cycle times Usage Rate for each item. If a product line is reviewed just once a month, you must buy at least 1 month's worth of every stock item. EOQ's answer might have been less.

5. Override EOQ when the item is seasonal. Instead, compute an order quantity to cover expected usage for the next three months (Remember the chapter on Seasonal items).

6. Override EOQ when a quantity price discount schedule for this individual item has been entered into the computer files. The fact that this schedule exists says: "You get a better price

by buying more. Use the evaluation technique to find the best quantity this time."

7. On certain items, program "shelf-life limits." If a product goes bad after six months, you must not allow EOQ to cause an 11-month-supply purchase.

8. Watch out for low-usage items. If you move $1/2$ unit or less per month (6 total for the year), *no formula* will do an effective job on ordering controls. Set the controls manually and freeze them until the usage picture changes. We'll talk more about this also in the next chapter.

9. When an item out in the branch is resupplied from your central warehouse, "Min/Max" is likely better than Order Point/Line Point/EOQ as the control method. Remember Chapter 6. The "Push" concept develops a replenishment quantity under logic different from EOQ's.

10 Override EOQ on blanket purchase order release quantities. If you've ordered 120,000 from the supplier, to be delivered 10,000 per month, the logic behind your decision has nothing to do with the factors EOQ considers. This too is discussed in Chapter 10.

11. Initial stocking quantities, when a product line is first taken on, should be conservative. EOQ is effective only after you have a track record on the products.

12. The logic for buying ahead of a price increase or in support of a promotion is not EOQ's logic. A completely different set of considerations helps answer these purchase quantity questions.

AVOID THE "STUPID" RECOMMENDATION

All these "fences" and overrides are programmed to keep your system from recommending some buying decision that common sense says is downright stupid. One of the reasons much of the software now on the market for distributors is largely ineffective in replenishment control functions . . . and the reason the buyers use their SWAG instead . . . . is that the systems often tell the buyer to do something that he or she knows isn't right. Once the buyer identifies one of these bad recommendations, you can imagine what he thinks from then on about the system:

> "When do I trust this system and when do I have to use my own judgement? Last week it recommended that I purchase 12 months supply of a seasonal item just as the season ended. It followed that piece of brilliance with a suggestion to buy 16 of an item when we're selling 400 per month. The next report advised me to bring in 300 . . . when I already have a blanket order in the file with scheduled releases of 2,000 per month. Shoot, this system is worthless. I'm going to make up my own mind what to do and override the thing every time I buy."

THE LOW-ORDERING POSITION ADJUSTMENT

While on the subject of avoiding the stupid recommendation, let's discuss an adjustment required when you're late in ordering . . . and surprisingly, this adjustment is missing from the logic of some software today. Here's the scene: Because of an unusually large sale, a popular stock item is well below the Order Point when the computer alerts you to place a purchase order for replenishment material. You certainly didn't intend for this to happen . . . but it has. Trouble looms on the horizon. The obvious first step is to call in the order and try every way possible to expedite the shipment from your supplier. Unfortunately, the supplier replies: "Gosh, I'm sorry about this Harry. It's still going to be the normal three weeks before we can ship." Now what? Well, one thing's pretty certain . . . you're almost surely going to run out of stock on the item. The Order Point is the *lowest position* an item should have dropped to before an order is placed. If you go well below that before ordering, you can count on a stockout unless special expediting can shorten the lead time.

Backorders from Customers Often Accumulate

In some cases, the stockout is real trouble. Customers won't wait. If you don't have the stuff, they just go elsewhere. The sales are lost. However, often they'll permit some delay in shipment if it's not too excessive, so they allow you to place their requirement on back-order. Trouble is . . . by the time replenishment stock arrives, the backorder buildup is sizable. Guess what happens when your purchase order shows up? Right . . . backorders eat up the entire quantity. You're right back in the soup. But this time, it's worse. You're not only ordering late, you have no stock at all.

A Bad Cycle Turns into a Tailspin

If this cycle repeats the next time material is received, and the next, . . . which it might if you don't act properly . . . what happens to this item? The problem goes away. Who corrects it for you? The customers. They just stop trying to buy this item from you, and there are no sales at all. You can play "ostrich" if you dislike unpleasant situations. Just don't do anything at all. The problem will go away. Very soon, *you* will too . . . . as the Boss gives you an opportunity for a new career path. If you'd like to continue in your current employment, corrective action is necessary.

Two Ways to Correct the Problem

Computer programming can help you pull out of this tailspin. There are two methods:

1. Increase the order quantity on the first P.O. when you must order in a position below the Order Point.
2. Trigger a second order for replenishment stock when you see that the backorder buildup has exceeded the incoming order quantity on P.O. Number 1 . . . even before the material has arrived.

Recommendation: Use Method Number 1. Get a jump on the problem by increasing the first order quantity right at the outset. Make the increase large enough to cover all expected backorders while you're out of stock . . . so that the regular order quantity puts you back into "sync." Yes, I *know* you're not out of stock right now. I realize that there are no backorders yet . . . but there will be! You're anticipating the stockout and the backorder buildup. You're "shocking" your system with extra material to cover these backorders, so that they do not exhaust all the incoming material.

How Much Should the Adjustment Be?

Add to the normal order quantity an amount equal to:

1. How much you're below Order Point, plus . . .
2. Half the difference between Line Point and Order Point

Example:

Normal EOQ = 150

Line Point ———————————————— 300

Order Point ——————————————— 200

$\uparrow$

ⓧ Item Position . . . . $\downarrow$ 110 units below Order Point

Safety
Allowance ——————————————— 50

Zero Stock ——————————————— 0

Order the normal EOQ 150
Add on the amount below Order Point 110
Add on one-half of Line Point—Order Point 50

Recommended Replenishment Quantity Now 310

What's the Basis for This Odd Adjustment?

This adjusted order quantity "pretends," in effect, that you were at the mid-point between Line Point and Order Point as this purchase order goes in to the supplier. That would have been a safe, solid position from which to start the replenishment process on this item. You're not there, of course, and a stockout is a probability. However, by adding on this difference from where you are and where you wish you were, you're preparing for a rash of customer backorders during the out-of-stock period.

No . . . you won't have stock when the customers first order, but you'll have an extra large quantity arrive from the supplier when the P.O. being placed today does show up. You can *cover all the waiting backorders* without exhausting the incoming stock. The regular EOQ . . . or whatever . . . then restores the item to a regular pattern. The regular order quantity is still available to handle customer needs anticipated on out ahead. Had you brought in only the EOQ with no increase, the waiting backorders might have taken it all . . . and that pattern repeated a time or two puts you out of business on this item.

Is This Necessary on Every Item?

This "Low-Ordering-Position" adjustment is needed only for the upper class stock items: Classes 1, 2, and 3. These are your stock items with the most dollars passing through the inventory, and therefore the normal ordering quantities are smaller . . . in terms of months' supply. You want higher inventory turns on these high-dollar-volume items. The smaller order quantities get the job done.

These items, however, are more susceptible to stockouts when something does go wrong. Yes . . . you *must* take that risk. You can't afford the inventory required to play it super-safe with this group. The Line Points and Order Points are designed to provide a very high customer service level . . . even with the high risk. Still, with their high volume, a stockout is more likely to generate the customer backorder buildup we've been discussing. The quick-turn order quantities, when they do arrive, are more likely to be eaten up.

Items in Classes 4 through 12 are those with ever-decreasing dollar volumes passing through the inventory. They don't have to be turned as often, and their normal replenishment quantities represent from four to twelve months' supply. EOQ develops similar quantities. When you're bringing in six months' supply of a stock item, for example, as the regular replenishment quantity . . . and you have a stockout period . . . it's not very likely that customer backorders will eat up the entire six months' supply when the stuff does show up. You may have to reorder a bit sooner than expected next time, but there's no immediate hazard. The normal EOQ will be able to fill all waiting backorders and still leave you with plenty of stock. The low-ordering position adjustment isn't needed on items in Inventory Classes 4 through 12.

Be Sure to Tell the Buyer about the Adjustment

In the adjustment example earlier, the suggested quantity to purchase wound up as 310. The "Recommended Replenishment Action Report" shows 310 as the amount to buy . . . but our Buyer is fairly new. Linda's been in her job only 30 days and is still trying very hard to grasp all these new concepts and controls. EOQ was a real puzzler, but she's beginning to understand it. She was quite proud of herself this morning when, for this item, she figured an EOQ on her desk calculator and got 150 . . . which is what the inquiry screen shows as the correct EOQ. She had a cup of hot chocolate to celebrate her new mathematical skills.

Now the computer prints a fresh report on this product line, and the suggested purchasing quantity for this item is 310. "What's going on?," Linda asks. "Has the stupid machine gone haywire? Why is it telling me to order 310 when the system EOQ is 150? Shoot, I thought I understood this stuff, but now I wonder if I ever will."

Codes to Explain Adjustments

Had the computer simply printed an "X" (or something) by the 310 quantity, and then explained at the bottom of the page what the "X" means . . . that the normal ordering quantity was increased because of a low ordering position . . . Linda knows what's happening and why 150 was not the suggested quantity to purchase. Her faith in the system and in her new-found knowledge is supported.

Remember to follow this counsel whenever the system overrides or adjusts the regularly-calculated order quantity. Use as many codes as you need. Select codes to handle several adjustments:

Code:

Y — The calculated order quantity exceeded 1 year's supply, and was decreased back to that limit.

TW — The calculated order quantity was less than 2 weeks' supply, and was increased up to that amount.

S — The item is seasonal. The suggested quantity represents expected usage for the next three months.

RC — This adjustment brought the order quantity up to the Review Cycle times the Usage Rate.

SL — The quantity is restricted by a shelf-life limit.

LB — (Line Buy). The computer increased this item's suggested buy quantity, proportionate with all others on the order, to enable you to place a $5,000 total order with this supplier . . . and thus save the freight.

X — This was a low-ordering-position adjustment, etc.

Use the codes you like . . . not necessarily the ones above. In each case, it helps the buyer to understand what the system is doing. She receives guidance to do the right thing instead of blindly following a calculation concept that may have drifted off course . . . and she *understands* what's going on.

The Adjustment for Order-Point-Only Items

Most distributors have some items that are the "stand-alone" type. Each item, purchased by itself, easily meets the supplier's ordering requirement. No "Line Buy" is required. Nothing else need be added to an order for the one item to qualify for the supplier's best pricing. Example: The supplier requires a $25 minimum purchase. He offers no better pricing for buying anything more than that. You stock four items of his . . . and it's very easy to buy at least $25 of each one when resupply is necessary. An Order Point . . . alone . . . is calculated for each of the four products. Line Points are unnecessary.

When one of the four gets caught down below Order Point at the time of replenishment, an adjustment is needed just as with items using both an Order Point and Line Point. How much? For them, my suggestion is to add-on the number of units below Order Point to the normal replenishment quantity. Again, this is needed only for the upper class products (1's, 2's, and 3's). The adjustment isn't necessary on Class 4 through 12 items.

Avoid Software That Still Lacks These Adjustments

NOW do you see why I'm so concerned about software houses with only a meager grasp of all this and have programmed EOQ's for use across the board? No overrides. No fences. No adjustments. "Graham likes EOQ. You say you want Graham's ideas. OK, you got it!" There's *no formula on the planet* that handles all items alike in every condition. You should now have a good checklist of conditions the software must be able to handle properly, if you're to be a prospect. When you mention some of these overrides or adjustments and the salesman says, "Gosh, we've never run into that problem before. But I know we can change our system to handle it." . . . *run,* do not walk, away from that outfit.

THE "K" AND "R" COSTS . . . REVISITED

Before we leave this chapter and move on to other weird topics, let's revisit our old friends . . . the "K" Cost, which you'll remember is the annual cost of carrying inventory . . . and the "R" Cost, how much your company spends each time you go through the replenishment cycle on a stock item. Both are part of the EOQ calculation, and "K" is considered in other analyses also. Both are sometimes miscalculated. When they are, the order quantity answers are incorrect and maybe even damaging to use.

The Correct "K" Cost

As my old boss Bob Van De Mark used to say, "Too many distributors want to joust with minutia . . . instead of spending their time on the important stuff." Bob liked strange words. What he meant, I'm sure, is: "Don't get so caught up trying to dot i's and cross t's, that you forget what you're writing." There's a danger here with the "K" Cost.

Some distributors try to compute one that considers every possible aspect of carrying stock. In fact, they develop a different figure for each branch and sometimes even one for different items. Their logic:

> "Hey . . . our warehouses are of differing sizes, in different labor markets. Some are new, some old, and they're not all worth the same amount per square foot. The items we stock vary all over the place in size, cost, and risk of theft. It makes sense to work out a different Carrying Cost Percentage by branch, and sometimes even for certain items."

While all this is true, it's simply not worth the trouble to develop, maintain in the computer, and use different K's . . . and also spend the time required to make sure the right one is always applied to the right branch or item. There are *much* more important problems to address first, given the limited time distributors have to work on inventory headaches. An example? The accuracy of shelf counts on stock items versus the computer records! Boy, inaccuracies there hurt you far more than does a slightly-off K Cost. Why not devote max effort to "Day's-Work-In-A-Day" and Cycle Counting . . . before losing sleep over the K being off 2%.

Recommendation: Use One "K" Cost for the Company

Avoid such needless "jousting." Calculate a single K Cost Percentage about once each year, hard code that number into the computer, and apply it everywhere, on every item, in every required calculation. The short-cut method is simply to take the current Prime Rate of borrowing money and add another 20% onto that. Example:

$$
\begin{array}{lr}
\text{Current Prime Rate} \dotfill & 10\% \\
\text{Increment For All Other Cost Factors} \dotfill & \underline{20\%} \\
\text{K Cost} \dotfill & 30\%
\end{array}
$$

That short-cut approach yields a very effective K Cost for most distributors. If you actually try to dig into all your cost records, the answer might be way off. K includes costs of a very "gray" nature . . . expenses that are mixed into many others and not separated or identified clearly on any operating statement. It's easy to make a mistake, so use the recommended short-cut method and develop a K that's well within an acceptable range. Use that K Cost for every branch and for every item.

When a football team can't block or tackle, it isn't a productive exercise for the coaching staff to spend many hours trying to decide whether they should wear shoes with $1/2''$ or $3/4''$ cleats. Yes . . . they need cleats. If they've got 'em, spend the available time on blocking and tackling fundamentals.

THE "R" COST *CAN* BE DIFFERENT FOR SOME ITEMS

The cost of going through a replenishment cycle . . . the "R" Cost . . . is different. It certainly can vary from item to item. In my earlier book, I really didn't touch on this point. Instead, like the K, I recommended that one "R" be applied companywide. Well, times change. Conditions in distribution do as well. What might have been true a few years back may need modification as distributors move into new markets, become "processors," start buying more from overseas sources, and begin applying bar coding for improved accuracy. The $5 "R" Cost recommended earlier still applies most of the time. Here's when it does:

> If a stock item coming through your Receiving steps is taken straight to the warehouse shelf . . . and nothing at all is done to it physically . . . then $5 is the figure to be used as that item's "R" Cost.

Of course, for many wholesale distributors, that rule covers almost every item they stock. It did in years past. It will in years to come . . . although the $5 will likely go up as overall costs increase in the future. Today, though, there are a growing number of exceptions.

Bar Coding

Bar Coding receives an overview in Chapter 14, but for now let's just say that bar coding has come on strong over the last few years.

It's logical. It improves accuracy in receiving, warehousing, order-filling and shipping. Item identification errors are reduced, employee productivity is increased, and steps like Cycle Counting or physical inventory at year end are much more efficiently performed. The cost vs. savings ratio is very positive. It just took a little while for the concept to "settle down" to fewer codes, better and cheaper equipment, and wider acceptance.

Perhaps you're heavily into bar coding already, but quite a number of products arrive from your suppliers either uncoded or with a code you can't use. You have to apply bar codes to each item or each box before moving the material into the warehouse and putting it away. If you haven't included the labor cost of doing this in the unit cost of the items involved, then that labor goes into the "R" . . . the Cost of going through a Replenishment Cycle. Such items might have an "R" of $25 instead of only $5.

Repackaging Steps

How about the fastener distributor who buys in large bulk quantities overseas? Each time a shipment arrives, his first step is to repackage the screws, nuts, washers, bolts or whatever, into boxes of 100 or shrink-wrapped packs of 50. The labor in this case is pretty substantial, and certainly I'd recommend that it be included in the "landed cost" of each product. If for some mystical reason you choose not to . . . then increase each item's "R" cost to about $50.

Do you see the principle? A $5 "R" Cost is just fine when you *don't do anything* to the item after receipt. It simply goes as is straight out the door on a backorder or onto the warehouse shelf. If, however, you perform some type of labor on it . . . bar coding, repackaging, kitting, plating, cutting, painting, converting in any form . . . *every time* before it's available for sale, then use an increased "R" Cost for the item. This too is logical. It *does* cost your company more to go through a replenishment cycle on such items than on those that are stocked and sold in the exact condition received. You'll get more profitable EOQ's with more accurate numbers in the formula.

SUMMARY

EOQ . . . the Economic Order Quantity formula . . . is an old, well-worn, time-tested tool. It's also much maligned. Many "forward-thinkers" today say that it's outlived its usefulness. They see it as stodgy and old-fashioned, and push the wholesale distributor toward "DRP" (Distribution Requirements Planning) or some other mutation out of manufacturing. Trouble is . . . we're not manufacturers. We're not in the "Physical Distribution" business either (the manufacturer sending his products out to the market through his own controlled warehouses). We're *wholesale distributors* . . . a strange breed indeed, but one with unique headaches that the mutations don't address. EOQ still serves very well when used correctly.

Recognize that the carpenter's hammer hasn't had a basic design change in 60 years or so. Why? Because it solves some problems quite well. Yes, there are air-hammers, electric staplers, and so on . . . but every carpenter still carries around his old standby. There are some problems that only the basic-design hammer can handle. That's true of EOQ. It too solves basic order-quantity problems in certain conditions better than anything else. Yes, even in the 21st century.

But EOQ is also abused. It's sometimes used improperly or with bad information feeding its formula, and of course the results are poor or even worse . . . disastrous. The critics jump in quickly: "See . . . I *told* you not to trust that dusty formula. Now look what its done to you!" Hmmm . . . ask the carpenter what happens when the hammer is used in a screwdriver application. How effective is it when he holds the wrong end and pounds away? What occurs when the handle breaks on a downstroke? Sure . . . trouble. It's that way with *any* tool applied improperly or not "maintained" in a safe manner. Be sure you build in the fences, overrides, adjustments and correct information. Use EOQ only where it fits. You'll like the profit it generates for you.

Purchasing Variations and Aberrations 10

One gripe about Inventory Control methodologies in the past was that they tried to apply the same logic . . . the same controls . . . to every stock item in every condition. I remember arguing the point with a boss once: "No one formula works all the time." Certainly I don't want you to fall victim to that trap as you apply the Graham concepts. I offer what I believe to be sound counsel in computing usage rates, lead times, order points, line points, EOQ's, Inventory Classes and the like. These control methods and formulas work most of the time for the durable goods distributor on most of his stock items. They do not work every time in every condition. The variations necessary for seasonal items were discussed in Chapter 4. More modifications were covered in the last chapter as fences, overrides and adjustments to EOQ. We're not through. Some of those exceptional conditions of the last chapter deserve more than a casual mention. Then there are old buying habits that distributors should trash once and for all . . . and there are even more special conditions that haven't been brought up so far. While we're at it, let's get into them too.

THE SQUEEZE ON DISTRIBUTORS

Today, distributors are squeezed from both ends of their business. Customers demand lower prices but with premium service. Many are reducing the number of distributors from whom they buy . . . drastically . . . and there's serious hurt to those distributors who don't make the cut. Competition is fierce. Larger distributors keep getting even bigger by acquisitions, spreading into more and more markets, wielding their huge buying power like a bulldozer if the smaller guy meets them head on.

Suppliers are reducing the number of distributors they'll authorize . . . going for the larger, better-managed, more-stable, higher-potential outfits, instead of the 1970's approach of "sign up everybody." They encourage larger purchases. They want distributors to assume more of the inventory load for a region and carry a wider range of products locally. And their prices keep climbing steadily . . . sometimes vacillating a bit during changing economic climates . . . but always up in the long run.

The average-size distributor has only a few defenses for such a squeeze. One is a higher productivity level per employee . . . as we discussed in some of the earlier chapters. If he works smarter, more efficiently, with less errors, with fewer but better people and a superior computer to assist, then he can sell at prices in line with his giant competitor and still survive. Another ploy is to specialize so narrowly, or in such a remote geographic area, that the big guy sees little advantage to competing in his specialty or market. He can charge higher prices. Nobody else can perform this function . . . or at least not within 200 miles. If this wouldn't work for you, there are other countermeasures available: Systems Contracts and Blanket Orders.

THE SYSTEMS CONTRACT

There's no intent here to represent myself as an expert in Systems Contracting. I'm not. Others like Ralph Bolton in East Amherst, New York (716) 688-8394 and Norman St. Cyr in Danvers, Massachusetts (508) 777-0976 are true specialists in this area. If you really want to find out the best approaches to Systems Contracting, contact one of them. My point here simply is this: Systems Contracts offer a chance to "lock up" a segment of business for a time period. The customer agrees to buy a particular item, in a specified total quantity sometimes with set release amounts, over a defined time frame, and until changed . . . at a given price.

"Dependent" or Known Demand

The distributor can now count on several things:

1. What business there is from this customer on this item or group of products is *his* for the contract period.
2. There are some groundrules. He knows the total quantity he'll have to provide for the contract and usually the expected release quantities and timing. He must be able to deliver 200 at any time, but no more than 400 in one week, 10,000 for the year, etc.
3. Pricing is set. Hopefully, he's negotiated the right to raise a price during the contract with 30 days notice and documented verification of a cost increase from his supplier. However, he can't always do that. The customer may have agreed to the deal to lock-in prices for the contract period.
4. His service level on the contract items must be 100%, or pretty doggone close, if the customer doesn't violate the release-quantity and timing limits. At times, there are penalty clauses built in if he doesn't deliver as contracted. The customer may procure the item from any source, at any price, by any transport method . . . and the distributor has to make up the price difference.

A Blanket Order to a Supplier Covers the Contract Requirements

The demand expected on the contract items changes from "Independent" to "Dependent" . . . or Known Demand. With the advantage of knowing what to expect ahead of time, the distributor may also do some "locking-in." Rather than replenishing a contract item under an Order Point/Line Point/EOQ system (controls designed to handle "Independent" or unknown demand), the distributor places blanket orders with suppliers for at least the high-volume items in the contract. The supplier gets an order for 10,000 units . . . 1,000 to be released the 1st of each month. The distributor, like his customer, now has assurance of a continuity of supply at set costs.

Special P.O. Numbering for the Blanket Helps Later Control Steps

Every edge you can gain to prevent lost motion is worthwhile. I've found that if you'll number the blanket purchase order releases separately, it allows the computer to treat each release as a separate P.O. Control steps like expediting, re-scheduling a release, processing a supplier's invoice . . . all are much easier when the computer can isolate one release from another. The blanket purchase order numbering might look like this:

Original P.O.	100,000 units P.O. Number 24500-00
Release 1 for Jan. 1	10,000 units P.O. Number 24500-01
Release 2 for Feb. 1	10,000 units P.O. Number 24500-02
Release 3 for Mar. 1	10,000 units P.O. Number 24500-03
Etc.	

A "covering" blanket order number 24500-00 for 100,000 gets the pricing set. The supplier is instructed to release 10,000 each month in accord with the following pages. Each attached page carries a different P.O. number suffix, and is keyed into your computer such that the machine thinks you placed ten different P.O.'s. The supplier is asked to invoice each release by the full P.O. number, including the correct suffix.

You can now develop special programming to monitor each release independently a certain number of days ahead of the scheduled ship-date. Let's say that the supplier agrees to a 30 day "window" ahead of each date . . . in which you may move the ship-date up or back as much as two weeks, or you may change the quantity up or down by 50%. He may even let you cancel one release somewhere during the ten months. Changes like these could prove very helpful if the customer moves faster or slower than planned on his end. To do this, however, the computer must consider each release apart from the others.

In similar fashion, a supplier's invoice applies clearly to a particular release. It can get pretty confusing as to what you owe, what you've already paid, what happened exactly if a shipment was shorted or doubled-up . . . if all invoices simply carry the covering blanket order number.

Blanket Orders Are Exceptions for Many Distributors

There's nothing very mystical about blanket orders. Some distributors use them all the time. Others need them infrequently. If you just use them rarely, then this section was a sure cure for your sleep disorder. You might do well to consider them more often. A distributor told me recently that he bought over $1 million a year from a supplier who required only a $2,000 order to get the best prices. He should approach that manufacturer with an offer to buy $50,000 at a time and then negotiate special pricing that his (apparently) abnormal buying power should earn.

But if you're an old hand with blankets, my point is simply: Order Points and EOQ's, etc., are out of their element in this situation. They don't apply except for the lower-volume items in the contract . . . and even with these, you should increase the expected usage rates to include the contract numbers if you didn't sell these items to this customer last year. Be careful *not* to permit a person or your computerized system to apply the wrong control when conditions call for something entirely different . . . as with this next condition: The "dominant" stock item.

FLOW POINTS

A few distributors sell one or two items in such fantastic volume that the critters must get a very high inventory turn rate . . .

much higher than normal ordering controls would develop. The items aren't normal at all. They're "dominant," in that they make up an unusually high percentage of the overall sales volume. For example, a paper distributor in St. Louis sells tremendous quantities of paper towels. They buy two or three truckloads a week of the stuff to generate inventory turns of about 100 per year. It's a low-profit item, but the higher turns make it worthwhile. Besides, if they didn't offer this item at a competitive price, the customers would assume they're about to go out of business. A "Flow Point," rather than an Order Point-Line Point-EOQ combination, is the control suited to this stock replenishment situation. Here's how it works:

- The distributor expects to move out virtually all stock on the item one or more times each week.

- The targeted quantity he therefore expects to find out in the warehouse each Friday afternoon is very low: Perhaps only 20 cases . . . a small buffer, or to play it super-safe, a full truckload held in reserve.

- His supplier is set up to deliver a full truckload each Monday, Tuesday, and Wednesday. If he doesn't get a call from the distributor by late Friday, the truck scheduled for Monday is sent on its way.

- The distributor may call Thursday, however, and ask for two trucks Monday. He may call late Friday and say that only two trucks are needed the following week. For this to work, the supplier must be totally reliable. He *will* show up on the schedule unless instructed otherwise.

- A "flow" is set in motion, just as you'd turn on a faucet. But the supplier allows the distributor to increase or decrease this flow on very short notice for the next week's shipments.

- The "Flow Point" is that 20 cases of buffer or the truckload reserve. The flow is turned up or down based on the stock position relative to the 20 at the date and time of "control."

Keep the Flow Point Item Out of Your Classification Exercise

Just a little point here about these very high-volume items. When you classify to find a branch's Class 1 through 12 items, keep the flow point items out of the exercise. You have no intention of handling them as Classification would dictate, and if left in, they "skew" the classes badly. The only distributors who ever call me about problems with Classification are those who've included the very high-volume items . . . or perhaps have failed to eliminate the real dogs at the opposite end of the usage spectrum. Classes 1 through 12 are effective if you keep the super fast-moving and super-slow items out of the exercise which assigns the class to each item.

THE LARGE DISTRIBUTOR'S ALTERNATIVE TO REVIEW CYCLES

As mentioned earlier, there are some really large distributors evolving these days. Others have been in the "giant" category for many years. My definition of a giant is a distributor with sales of $100 million or more per year. These guys have tremendous buying power with many of their suppliers, and most have large central/regional warehouses or buying centers. They have very little trouble placing purchase orders that meet a supplier's requirement for "last-column pricing." Some of these outfits could place qualifying orders almost every day. Product line "Review Cycles," as discussed in my earlier book, need modification if they're to be helpful.

Each Morning Brings New Purchasing Decisions

Instead of using only a planned purchasing cycle for a supplier, the large distributor programs different features to supplement the cycle concept. The first thing each morning after a buyer arrives (following a trip to the coffee bar), he asks the computer to display the status of all product lines assigned to him. He's looking for those that should be purchased today. The information returned looks something like this:

Today's Date: Sept 1

Product Line	Total Required	Item Count At OP	Item Count Below OP	Item Value Below LP	Next Planned Purchase	Buy Today
Ajax	5,000 P	0	0	2,200 P	Sept 10	
BRX	10,000 $	1	0	10,300 $	Sept 4	X
Consol	1,000 U	0	0	300 U	Sept 15	
DX	5,000 $	2	1	4,800 $	Sept 3	X
Front	20,000 P	0	0	21,250 P	Sept 6	X
GRD	1,500 P	1	1	1,312 P	Sept 1	X

P = Pounds $ = Dollars   U = Units

In a dynamic, high-volume distributor, the ability to meet supplier total-order purchase requirements changes daily. Often they can buy a product line today that would have required too much "stretching" yesterday. Yes, they plan an approximate date for the next P.O. for each supplier, but each morning they review the new status of all lines . . . to decide which ones justify purchasing action *today*. Line Points may be set based on the planned purchasing cycle for each line, but as you see above, three product lines should be purchased now . . . ahead of the planned date. Only one line (the last) is right on schedule. Two other product groups need no action right now. They seem to be tracking along toward their next scheduled purchase date about as planned.

The Buyer Now Tells the Computer What to Do

Those X's you see above in the last column would have been keyed on the screen by the buyer after reviewing all the information. The buyer is instructing the computer:

"OK machine, now print out for me the Recommended Replenishment Action Reports for the product lines I've marked. I'll look them over and then get back to you, item by item, on what I want you to do next."

In a few minutes, the buyer receives the reports back and decides what to do on every item listed. He may transfer-in surplus on some from other locations; he may seek permission to substitute one brand for another for a while; he may go ahead and purchase everything from the supplier. Those are the options every buyer faces regardless of when his reports print out. The point stressed here: In a heavy-volume environment, the buyer decides *each morning* which product lines he'll work on that day . . . rather than waiting for the review cycles to run their courses, as does the smaller distributor with limited buying power who has the computer print out automatically the Action Reports for each day on more of a planned basis.

AN OLD PURCHASING CONCEPT THAT NEEDS TO BE BURIED

Now that we've covered some variations to normal controls, let's move on to a purchasing "aberration." Amazingly, I still see distributors buying this way when I thought the practice had gone out about the same time as drive-in movie theaters. Drive-in's served a useful purpose (remember the steamed-up windows?). This buying concept never was effective. Today, it's not only outdated . . . it's harmful. The technique? "10th Prox Purchasing." The logic:

> "Buy everything you can so that the material arrives after the 25th of the month. The supplier's billing cycle and payment terms are such that we'll have an extra 30 days to pay for the stuff. We'll use his money for 30 extra days."

A tiny piece of the logic is OK: You will delay the required payment by 30 days. Instead of having to pay for the material by the 10th of April, for example, payment for anything coming in after March 25 gets pushed back to May 10th. It isn't worth it. There are too many negatives.

A Big Group of Headaches Descend on You

When you buy this way, a "wave" of work hits your company. The Receiving crew works like beavers the last week of the month and looks for something to do the rest of the time. The warehouse employees who put merchandise away do the same thing. Accounts Payable personnel are up to their ears when all the invoices arrive at once. Purchasing, too, really has to work hard in only a short burst to get all the orders in under the groundrules. Remember the earlier discussions about productivity and its importance to your survival in the future. This purchasing approach has lousy employee productivity built in.

What's worse . . . you have to carry *extra inventory on every item all the time* to permit this buying practice. You have to build up your stock to a fat position, since you're waiting longer than really necessary to begin replenishment on many items. You've introduced an alien factor into the replenishment-timing decision . . . something that has **nothing to do** with the problem. Customers dictate usage rates; suppliers control lead times. Those are the only factors to be considered. Both are external. Both are outside of your control and thereby preclude any effort to arbitrarily manipulate them. With this buying method, you've plugged-in an internal factor.

But What about That Extra 30 Day's Use of the Money?

What's gained? Frankly, you get a one-time use of the supplier's money for the extra 30 days. After that, you have to keep on buying this way to simply maintain your advantage . . . and what's 30 days' use of his money really worth? With the prime rate at 10%, let's say, then one month extra saves you less than 1%. What's the carrying cost of inventory . . . even without the financial investment cost? As I write, it's about 20% per year: A little more than $1^{1}/_{2}$% per month. It costs you $1^{1}/_{2}$% to save 1%, and you have to keep spending the $1^{1}/_{2}$% month after month for your *one-time* 1% saving. With more logic like that, you'll soon be a non-profit organization but without the tax benefits.

That's why this purchasing concept was trashed long ago by distributors who understood what they were doing. Yes, I know that there are times when you simply don't have enough cash to buy as

I've recommended. Adjustments are not only advisable . . . they're mandatory. The next chapter offers ways to pull cash out of inventory and the purchasing system in a crisis. Just don't do it by using the 10th Prox ("Look out for the wave!") method.

THE SAFETY ALLOWANCE . . . REVISITED

Attendees at my training sessions or who've watched the video course are sometimes argumentative about my approach to the safety allowance, which you'll recall is part of an order point calculation. Let's review the basic order point formula:

Order Point = (Usage Rate × Lead Time) + Safety Allowance

You'll recall how I suggest that you begin:

Order Point = (Usage Rate × Lead Time) + 50%

$$OP = (\quad 100 \quad \times \quad 1.0 \quad) + 50$$

$$OP = \quad 150$$

Yes, for all items as you kickoff a system, add 50% to the answer derived by multiplying monthly usage rate by the average lead time. All three elements together result in an order point. That 50% SA advice came from an analysis of answers when someone employs one of the many other safety allowance formulas available today . . . some of which are quite complex. An odd phenomenon occurs. 95% of the time, the complex formulas tell you to add between 25% and 75% as safety onto the basic usage rate times lead time calculation. My counsel: Jump right in the middle of where you'd wind up using the high-math approach, and get an answer that's understandable . . . one that Agnes can do in her head or on a hand calculator. Remember, even though the computer makes all the calculations, if Agnes doesn't understand how the answer was developed . . . either she won't follow the recommendation or she will every time like a robot.

What's the Point of Contention?

Old-time buyers reply one of two ways: "Gosh, that's *way* more safety than we carry now!" . . . or, "No way, Graham. We have to carry a *lot* more than that!" They see the 50% as either far too much or not nearly enough. Well, they can't both be right. The truth is: Neither should worry. They're just confused as to how this safety allowance concept compares to the way they might have thought of safety stock in the past.

Retire the "Days of Safety Stock" Method

The dusty old "Days of Safety Stock" concept is another one that should be put out to pasture. When a distributor sets out to keep 30 days of safety stock on all items, for example, it's like the government deciding that everybody should pay $10,000 a year Income Tax. Maybe that's not such a bad idea. It sure would simplify the process, but doesn't it make more sense to actually compute what each person owes? . . . then pay up. $10,000 is a nice, easy number to remember. It would be easier to calculate our returns. It's also expensive if it's wrong . . . either to the poor taxpayer or to Uncle Sam. Someone will really get hurt.

What happens when 30 days' safety stock isn't enough? You'll run out. If it's excessive, you'll carry way too much zero-turn inventory in that segment of each item's stock. How do you know when it's correct, when it's too much, when it's not enough? Sweeping, "Broad Brush" controls like this are easy to program and apply, of course, but the effect is costly. You can guess the overall inventory impact as time moves along. The broad brush number must be raised higher and higher to cover the items where 30 days won't cut it. More and more items now have incredibly excessive stock in the warehouse. Fantastic customer service results. So does bankruptcy.

The Calculated Safety Allowance Is Tailored to Each Item

If it takes a supplier a long time to ship material, it makes sense to protect for that with a higher overall order point, a portion of which would be higher safety stock. If the supplier proves extremely erratic, delivering in two weeks or two months with no predictable pattern, more safety stock should be added. An item with a highly erratic usage track record . . . you might sell 10 next month or 2,000 . . . also deserves more safety.

The Order Point formula above begins by developing differing safety stock quantities for higher usage and longer lead time items than the others. The 50% is a "by-product" of the usage rate times lead time calculation, so the answer naturally depends on those two numbers. Yes, it will have the effect of a certain number of days' worth in safety for each item . . . but a different amount for each one.

Adjustments Upward Are Made Item by Item

Certainly, I'll acknowledge that the beginning 50% answer isn't enough safety in some conditions. For most items, it's just fine. It generates a solid 90% service level (measured the correct way . . . read the 1987 book). I do recommend that it be increased on an item-by-item basis when very erratic usage is encountered, hit-or-miss suppliers must be used, or when a particular item is *so* important that it must be handled at a 98% service level.

This will sound like burn-at-the-stake-level heresy to your salesmen, but an excellent way to identify the items needing more than 50% safety is to run out of stock. It's true. There are nagging conditions possible with a stock item that are very hard to see ahead of time. Once they occur, however, a buyer can apply control corrections, freezes and the like which will reduce greatly the chances of it happening again.

In Line Buying Situations, You Have Some Hidden Help

The 50% safety allowance is plenty for most stock items for another reason. When you must buy the "truckload," for example, and this requires purchasing an assortment of the supplier's products . . . the average item when ordered isn't at the order point. It's somewhere above the order point (hopefully) but below the line point. Like this:

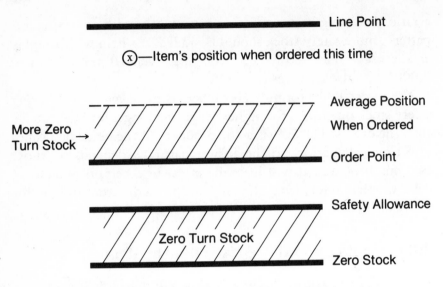

In fact, on the average, an item is halfway between line point and order point. Sometimes it's up closer to the line point; sometimes it's down next to the order point. On the average, it's halfway between. This has the effect of creating more zero-turn inventory for each item when it must be purchased with others like this . . . under Line Buying controls. This zero-turn material is what I call "Purchase-Order-Accumulation-Time" stock. It allows the buyer time to accumulate a purchase order large enough to meet the supplier's total-order requirement, get the order placed, and still have no item in the group any lower than order point . . . a tough juggling act for sure.

The normal 50% safety allowance is designed to avoid a stockout even when an item is all the way down to order point when replenishment is triggered. That full 50% must remain there for all items, since no one knows exactly which items will have dropped to order point when the next P.O. goes in to the supplier. The order point is the lowest acceptable position for an item when replenishment is initiated . . . but it is acceptable. The safety allowance allows any item in the product line to drop that low, even when we know that most won't be there when purchased.

This All Results in Extra Safety Stock

When an item is purchased under Line Buying controls, there's really more than 50% safety built in . . . on that item's average replenishment cycle. The item won't be down to order point on the average. It'll be at some level above. When that happens, more safety stock is actually provided for the item than 50%. Sometimes only a little more; sometimes quite a bit more. On the average, it's half the difference between line point and order point. That's why a starting safety allowance of 50% for most items is plenty, even when one has a mildly erratic usage or lead time history (which nearly all items have). Be careful about adding a lot more to safety just because it doesn't "feel" right, based on how you've operated in the past.

DON'T USE *ANY* FORMULA ON LOW-USAGE ITEMS

Sometimes I receive another complaint from companies attempting to apply my concepts: "Graham, your Order Point formula or that EOQ stuff doesn't work for us!" But when I press them for specifics, it isn't every item they stock that causes trouble. For many, the formulas and their adjustments/fences work just fine. The trouble-makers are often just those items with very low usage.

Remember: When an item has usage of less than $1/2$ unit per month . . . 6 for the year . . . then *NO FORMULA* can be used to effectively guide the replenishment timing and quantities. A human must set the controls arbitrarily and then freeze them in the computer, so that it does not recalculate and change them. For example, you might decide to sell the one unit on the shelf and then replace it. The Order Point is zero; the Order Quantity is 1. You lock those two controls into the computer with these programming instructions (in effect):

> "Listen machine, watch the status on this item. When we sell the one unit on the shelf, tell me and I'll order another one from the supplier. Don't ever change these numbers on your own, no matter how the sales pattern changes. Each month, however, give me a special report showing this and all other "frozen" items. Show me the usage pattern

for each one. I'll review the list to decide where to leave the controls alone, change them, or remove the "freeze" so that you can refigure the controls every month as you do for all other items."

You May Have More Items Like This Than You Thought

If a distributor carries 10,000 items total in stock . . . he might have 500 or more that need the human-set and frozen controls. 5% of his items have usages so low that they fall outside the range of formulized guidance. Obviously, if he tries to apply the formulas on these 500 anyway, the results are poor. Be careful with this. Any tool works only on the problems it's designed to handle. Don't throw out the hammer as useless when you applied it instead of the screwdriver which should have been used. Don't throw out effective ordering concepts like Order Points/Line Points/EOQ's if you've applied them to problems they were never designed to solve.

RESERVED OR PROTECTED STOCK

Let's move now out of the area of formula application and modification and dig into another of the troublesome problems facing many distributors. What's the best way to handle "protected" or "reserved" inventory, especially when you also carry the same item in regular stock?

Here's the scene: A customer requests (or demands) that you place a specified quantity of material aside in your warehouse designated for his use only. He must be able to walk out there with you at any time and see "his" stock neat, tidy and in full quantity. How can you make sure you'll have it all the time? How do you make sure someone doesn't rob some of his stuff to fill a regular order? How do you avoid a massive overstock (in total) on the item, since it's carried also in regular stock? Tough questions . . . leading to gray hair or bulk purchases of Rolaids. If the customer is important, you have little choice but to comply with his demand. It's easy, however, to handle this wrong and cause a calamity at either end: A stockout or costly excess.

Set a Few Groundrules When the Deal Is Arranged

Salesmen confronted with such a request from a big customer should be trained to do some negotiating on the details of the special-stock agreement:

A. Is is necessary to include in this arrangement items where you've never experienced delivery problems from us in the past out of our normal stock?

B. Could we instead of a special-stock agreement, work out a systems contract for the total quantity you expect to buy next year, with anticipated release dates and quantities . . . under which we agree to a 100% service level?

C. May we review your performance on the reserved products after six months and drop some from the agreement or reduce the quantities to be set aside?

D. If we can demonstrate an ability to service your needs from regular stock levels, may we discontinue the protected stock agreement at some point?

The customer may answer, "Absolutely not!" or "Yes, you must!" to every question. You're no worse off for having asked . . . and if he agrees to some of these conditions or alternatives, you've improved your ability to service him without carrying massive stocks that often get pretty dusty.

He Agrees to Nothing. You're Stuck. Now What?

If you must proceed without any relief on his conditions, what's the best way to administer the agreement? Well, the first step in my opinion is to segregate his protected stock physically in the warehouse and place it under tight control . . . perhaps with only one employee authorized to place material in or remove stock from the controlled area. Some distributors disagree with me on this, but my experience has been painful when I tried to leave such material unprotected and accessible to all employees. Oh sure, if the item is stocked *only* for this customer, such tight control isn't needed . . . but if you carry the same item in regular stock, you'd better cage up the reserved material.

I'm always nervous about a warehouseman (or worse, a salesman) out there looking for material to fill an order. The computer says we're out of stock, but he just wants to make sure so he's wandering around. He walks up on this protected stock with "ABC INDUSTRIES" name on the bin. Shoot, ABC isn't his account. You can guess what happens, and how bad you look the next time ABC orders the item. My point: If you agreed to a costly stocking arrangement like this, there must have been a good reason. You certainly want to perform well. Take all the precautionary measures necessary to assure that you don't foul up.

The Way *Not* to Program the Computer

Distributors who don't want to segregate the material argue that they can program the computer to handle this condition. They simply add the agreed-upon protected amount to each items safety allowance, like this:

$$OP = (\text{Usage Rate} \times \text{Lead Time}) + \text{Safety Stock} + \text{Reserved Quantity}$$

"See, Graham. We've got the full protected amount as extra safety stock. We can just leave the reserved stuff right in with regular material. There's always plenty for old ABC Industries." Hmmm . . . seems logical, and yes, most of the time you'll be OK. In fact, you may never get into trouble and be unable to ship the item when ABC orders. The reason? You've built a massive zero-turn segment of stock on this item. You've applied inventory "overkill."

The Special Customer's Usage Has Already Affected Safety Stock

This is beginning to get a little technical, and if you're sleepy, close the book and start again tomorrow. If you're alert and just had a cup of coffee, then stay with me on this. When all usage is lumped together in the computer's usage history for this item . . . both regular usage and ABC Industries . . . then the regular 50% safety allowance calculation considered ABC's sales as the number was generated. In theory, you don't need anything extra added to be able to take care of ABC's requirements any more than for any other customer . . . yet, to be sure, the full reserved amount was added as safety. The regular S.A. is designed to provide 90% service. Of course, for ABC it's to be 100% . . . so the add-on should do the trick. It will, and more. It's almost certainly *far too much* to carry in total. It's far beyond what is really needed to take care of ABC. There's a better way.

A Separate Part Number for the Protected Stock

To handle this smoothly, assign a separate part number to the protected stock segment:

Regular Stock Item: SKF 6203-2RS 0000   (Final 4 zeros not displayed)

Protected Item: SKF 6203-2RS 0020   (Final 4 digits are displayed)

Notice that the two numbers are the same through the first 10 digits. That's important. When the final four digits are "0000," that designates the regular stock item. "0020" means it's the normal item set aside just for ABC Industries. When programmed properly, the computer scans the condition of the other item when checking the status of its "mate." . . . but with a separate number, the computer maintains a totally different inventory and usage record on the protected material, apart from the regular stock. It has its own warehouse location, usage rate, order point, order quantity, and perhaps even a different cost. The replenishment controls may be set arbitrarily for the protected stock and then frozen: "Buy 100 when the stock drops to 50" . . . or "Buy 50 when we sell the 50 on the shelf."

What's the Advantage?

The separate record allows you to track what happens on the protected item totally apart from what's going on with the regular stock. The arbitrary (human-set) controls can be adjusted for the reserved material without any effect on the normal inventory. A picking ticket printed to fill an order from the protected-stock customer directs the order-filler to the location of the reserved material. When stock runs low, an option is presented. If sales on the regular material have slowed recently, you might elect to print a work order for the warehouse instructing them to pull from regular stock to replenish the special material . . . rather than ordering from the supplier. This isn't always wise to do of course, but once in a while the protected stock can help move out regular material that's hit the doldrums.

Less Total Inventory Is Needed

The major gain, however, is the average inventory required year-round to meet the protected-stock agreement conditions. When you isolate the track record on the reserved material from regular usage, you may then more-effectively set "Min's and Max's," or other arbitrary, non-calculated replenishment guidelines, to minimize the stock needed. Mixing the usage all together, as in the non-recommended method, requires a much higher safety allowance . . . much more zero-turn stock all the time . . . to guarantee that you'll be able to perform. True, the salesman for this account likes the "fat-safety-stock" method better, but his mourning period is quite brief if you file Chapter 11.

The Similar Part Numbers Offer Advantages in Programming

When the computer alerts the buyer that item SKF 6203-2RS should be replenished, the similar number SKF 6203-2RS 0020 appears also. The buyer sees the status of the protected stock. Perhaps that stock should be replenished now, rather than waiting for it to hit its minimum . . . and being unable to buy at a good cost. Conversely, if the protected stock drops to the minimum, the computer alerts the buyer to the status of the regular material. It may be purchased now, as well, or perhaps the special stock should simply be replenished from the regular inventory. The two part numbers are tied together. The computer is programmed to show the status of one when displaying information about the "mate."

An Opportunity to "Borrow" on Occasion

When a sales order is received on the regular stock, but it can't be filled, the computer displays the condition of the protected material. OK, I *know* the inside salesman isn't allowed to use that stock . . . but what if it's been gathering dust for six months with no activity at all? The Sales Manager should have the authority to do some "borrowing." Of course, you scramble to put the protected material back as soon as possible, but there's an excellent chance you can do that before ol' ABC Industries asks for some of that item. The four-digit suffix on the part number identifies the protected customer. If Ajax Industrial also wants that same item set aside for him, the part number on his stock is SKF 6203-2RS 0040. The normal stock, as you noticed earlier, was numbered SKF 6203-2RS (0000). The last four digits have no customer ID, so they're suppressed when the part number is printed or displayed. The final digits print or display only when they mean something.

SUMMARY

Are these ideas perfect solutions? I'm afraid not. This chapter offers only a few highlights to the full answers to very tough problems. Areas like systems contracting, blanket ordering, high-volume items, 10th-prox purchasing, human-set controls, and protected stock deserve their own independent books. Ralph Bolton and Norman St. Cyr have written extensively on the subject of systems contracting, for example, and you'd do well to read *their* books if you're heavily involved in this selling approach.

The exhortations here are to help you recognize conditions where the standard replenishment controls are out of their element, or to trash buying practices that introduce "alien" factors. Yes, much of this advice is common sense. Why do I feel a need to warn you? There are *still* software packages on the market today which don't address these problems. They employ numerous "defaults," especially when the system is first installed. In an effort to speed up the process, they start off the distributor with the same control concept on all items, all branches, all conditions. By trial and error, or after enough bad experiences, the distributor overrides many of the startup controls to force the system back to logical recommendations. But what happens if he doesn't know enough to do this effectively?

Or the software is the "loosey-goosey" variety mentioned in an earlier chapter. It never presumes to recommend any particular set of controls on any item or to offer guidance for an unusual condition. The buyer is expected to do his own thing on every item, every branch, every condition. If he or she knows what to do . . . fine. The "hooks" are built in to permit almost any control approach. Of course, if the buyer gets a bit lazy, isn't too skilled, or doesn't really know what to do, the system also permits wholesale defaults as directed by the buyer: "Just set a Minimum of 30 days stock; a Maximum of 60 days on all items. That'll work OK. It's the way we did it where I worked two years ago."

The days are long gone when you could survive with that level of non-professionalism lurking in your purchasing function encouraged by a free-wheeling computer system. When you're ready to buy your next system, look for one where the designers understand the exceptional situations of this chapter (and earlier). Get serious about packages only where the installers know enough to set up your system properly . . . the right type of controls for the right conditions . . . from the first day, and then can train your purchasing personnel to "fly" the wonderful new machine.

How to Reduce Inventory in a Crisis . . . But Without Crippling the Company

11

This chapter number sounds an ominous warning: Bad things lurk out there for any company who fails to act decisively when the "ox starts toward the ditch." To avoid Chapter 11, Management must first avoid the ostrich syndrome. Shoot, once in a while *every* distributor faces a crisis. A major account fails, owing you $700,000. A top profit-producing branch burns to the ground, or is ruined by a flood . . . and it'll be out of operation for over 60 days. You're nearing year-end . . . inventory tax-computation time . . . and the Boss walks in and commands: "We must get our inventories down $500,000 by December 31!"

Maybe the economy nosedives into an extended recession, and it becomes painfully apparent: Cash must be generated from *somewhere* or the company may not survive. Does one of these sound familiar? One thing is sure, you'll be a very unusual distributor if one or more of these little challenges doesn't afflict you by the early 21st century. The last chapter warned of one method to avoid when cash is short. Well OK then, what **should** you do?

The First Move

It can benefit you to simply panic. The rush of adrenalin you'll get as you contemplate unemployment, forced early retirement, or the consulting business may spur your brain to creative ideas. Trouble is . . . you've been doing a pretty good job with Inventory Management the last few years. There's some dead stock, but you've been attacking that cash-source consistently. Today, there's not much left to be "mined" from that vein. Inventory levels for most stock items, in most branch locations, are about where they should be. You're showing five to six true turns of the inventory each year . . . but regardless of all this, you *must* bring down the levels. The cash is needed elsewhere. How can you do it without wrecking your excellent service levels? How can you arbitrarily reduce inventory and still have customers left when the crisis passes?

The Short-Term Fixes Must Not Become a Way of Life!

Well . . . there are a few tricks. I almost hesitate to write this chapter and tell you what they are, however. Why? . . . for fear that you'll get all worked-up over the short-term results and adopt these tactics as your everyday mode of operation. Before we begin, let me sound this warning: **THESE ARE SHORT-TERM SOLUTIONS TO CRISES. THEY ARE NOT A WAY OF LIFE!** Yes, they'll generate much-needed cash. Yes, they'll improve turnover. But there **is** risk when these emergency procedures are used. The risk is calculated, and it's controlled for the most part . . . but it's still there. Key personnel will be adversely affected. It's important to keep to a minimum the time the company is exposed to the risks and the people strained.

The personnel involved in Purchasing and Inventory Management, as well as the Warehouse crew, must work considerably harder . . . perhaps even be overworked . . . on purpose for a limited time. Remember, there's a crisis. Survival just might be at stake. The boat is leaking . . . maybe to the point of sinking. Every crew member has to bail like crazy, even after they get tired. There are limits, though, as to how long they can be overextended.

A Parting Look at Dead Stock

There's one other point to be made before I open this box of magic tricks. Up above I made an assumption: You *have* dealt effectively

with slow-moving and dead inventory! If you haven't; if your program is a hit-or-miss, work-on-it-when-we-have-time effort; then stop. Take the time to read the chapter on the four-part dead stock disposition program in "Distribution Inventory Management For the 1990's." Dead Stock is **YOUR** first area for attack! Don't jump after these other techniques when your warehouse is full of stuff gathering dust!

A HIGHER INVENTORY CARRYING COST PERCENTAGE

Inventory Management professionals recognize that it does cost a bundle to carry merchandise in stock. Warehouse Space, Taxes, Insurance, Obsolescence, Theft, Damage, Material Handling, and the Value of Money Invested all represent dollars spent because you carry inventory. As I write, they add up to about 30 cents per year for every dollar carried (on the average) for a year in the warehouse. If you have $1 worth of stock on an item out in the warehouse all through the year, as an average, then there'll be 30 cents incurred as a total of all the carrying cost elements. Remember from Chapter 9, a short-cut way to determine this "K" Cost (mystic name for it) is to add 20% to the current commercial prime rate of borrowing money. Today, the prime is at about 10%. Adding 20% more gives a total "K" percentage of about 30%.

How the "K" Cost Is Used in Inventory Management

This 30% K Factor becomes an integral part of several formulas used to guide stock item replenishment. K is in the EOQ (Economic Order Quantity) formula. It's part of the individual item or total-order discount evaluation that finds which of several levels is the best for you to purchase; It's part of the formula for determining how much to buy before a supplier price increase or a promotion. The "Carrying" Cost is thus recognized as real . . . and potentially damaging to profits if too much merchandise is purchased at a time. Each formula lets the "K" have it's restraining effect . . . and that's good!

When the K percentage climbs, as when interest rates and other costs are rising, the restraining effect on inventory is greater. Replenishment stock quantities are reduced. Not as much is purchased. Lower discount levels are approved, rather than higher levels. The inventory turns faster to offset the higher costs involved in having it on the shelves.

Introduce a K Percentage That's Too High

So if you want to reduce your inventory smoothly . . . proportionately across all items . . . you can introduce a higher "K" percentage into these formulas. The correct K is 30%. You decide to use 40% . . . or 50%. What will happen to inventories? They'll come down. Not rapidly, not dangerously . . . but steadily and safely. Yes, safely . . . because it's not the quantity purchased that involves customer service. Service is controlled by **WHEN** replenishment is begun (the Order Points, Line Points, Minimums, etc.), and so far in this bag of magic tricks I haven't mentioned those. The order **quantities** are being reduced by a higher "K" percentage. The order points remain (for now) unchanged.

Playing games with the "K" percentage affects all items proportionately. You'll buy less of a Class 1 (very fast, high-dollar movement item), and less of a Class 12 (slow, small-dollar movement) . . . but what if that's not enough? Further reductions are needed.

BUY LESS OF THE LOWER-CLASS ITEMS

If you're familiar with EOQ's or an alternate approach . . . Buying By Inventory Class . . . you know that each method causes you to purchase from six to twelve months' supply of the slower-moving stock item at the time of replenishment. Of course, that's under normal conditions. This isn't a normal situation. The company's in trouble. Adjustments are required.

A second step then, after inserting the false K%, is to alter the calculated order quantities on the slower-moving items. Program the computer to cut them in half. Where you'd normally order six months' supply . . . order three. Where it would have been ten months' worth, cut that back to five. What happens? Smaller quantities arrive of course . . . even smaller than they would be as a result of the temporarily higher "K" cost factor.

Your warehouse people have to receive and put away quantities that are . . . frankly . . . too small on many items. The computer calls them up for replenishment more often than it should. Purchasing has to go through all the review and buying steps too frequently on such low-dollar-movement critters. Your administrative and warehouse people have to work much harder to keep up with the load . . . but remember why you're doing this: It's survival time. Cash must be repositioned out of inventory to other needs.

Be Careful Here. Don't Keep This Up too Long!

Maybe you can see the danger in these crisis-alleviation steps. The inventory comes down. Dollars **are** generated. "Boy, this feels good!," you reason. "Why not make these procedures a way of life around here? Think of the profit we'll make by operating with this 'forced-lower' inventory all the time!" *Don't do it! Don't even think about it!* Your key material control and handling personnel are being overworked . . . stretched very thin. They can stand up under the strain for 30 days . . . maybe even 60 . . . but they'll break down for sure if you prolong the arbitrarily-lower order quantities.

Yes, inventory is often your largest dollar asset. Your people, however, are your most important asset. There's a delicate balance every distributor tries to attain between the right number of people needed to perform a solid inventory management function and how much inventory is needed to provide a solid level of service to customers. The "K" factor and EOQ are both tools to help you achieve that balance. I've suggested here that you violate both, but that violation **must** be temporary . . . or you'll suffer more serious consequences than those causing you to take corrective action in the first place.

Watch the "Exhaustion Gauges" Carefully

You wouldn't drive your car much longer when the gauge shows it's overheating. It's an emergency situation so maybe you'll limp along for one more mile to that gas station up ahead, but continuing on to Houston is out of the question. A long-distance runner knows the signs that he's overextended his body and should drop out . . . and the smart ones do.

You'll see the signs in your people when you've gone far enough . . . errors they never made before; making excuses to not show up for work when that's uncharacteristic; arguments between departments that always got along well before; senseless, almost stupid errors in receiving, order-filling, and shipping; incorrect items added to purchase orders or omitted . . . things these competent people don't do normally. You've stretched them far enough. Back off! Return to the regular "K" Factor and the regular EOQ's . . . and give them a few days off if you can afford it.

TRUCKLOAD PURCHASES

Now I know that some distributors never buy a truckload of any-thing, but I'm using the term "truckload" purchase to represent all those total-order buys you're making now from many suppliers to qualify for free freight, an extra 5% off, etc., for the total purchase order. Some product lines are more competitive in your market than others. It's more critical to make these buys . . . save the discount, whatever form it takes . . . than for other product lines. On the critical lines, of course you continue to place the larger total-orders just as before the crisis. You have to. You can't afford an erosion of gross margin in these products.

Not Every Product Group Is in the "Make-or-Break" Category

What about the other product lines . . . those that are not so competitive? Perhaps on these lines, you *could afford* a lower gross margin for a while. Let's say you've been enjoying a 32% gross margin on a product line through volume buys. If you bought half as much in total at a time, you'd still be able to generate 25%. You can guess what you should do until the crisis passes: Sure, buy the lower total-orders on these lines. It will lower your inventory and generate much-needed cash.

PRE-SEASON BUYS, PROMOTIONS

Similarly, you might have to forego the usual big pre-season pur-chase of products in a highly-seasonal line. "Oh, no!," you scream. "That would really hurt us later on in the season when we don't have competitively-priced stock to sell!" Well, think that through a bit. There may not *BE* a season at all for you next Summer unless you take some serious steps now to get through this crisis! True, you have to do some things now that will have consequences later on, but first you have to make sure there's going to be a "later on." Next Summer, you'll still sell the products at competitive prices.

The gross margin will be lower. Right now, you must avoid paying out cash (you don't have or need elsewhere) for products that won't generate sales for several months.

Promotions

When economic times are tough, suppliers are affected too, and they in turn come up with more and more programs to increase their sales. Some of these promotional offers are **really** attractive. If you can avoid passing the savings on to your customers, the promotions offer chances for significant profit increases . . . but here too, you have to pick and choose. Last year perhaps, you would have loaded up in a particular product line and put on a heavy selling effort during the promotion. This year . . . for this product line . . . you can't.

I'm not advising you to pass up all promotional buying opportunities. Just as for the "truckload" purchases, you have to be selective right now. Jump on only the *best* promotions . . . those lines where you're strongest or where you'd be permanently damaged in the marketplace if you didn't participate. That's not the case in all lines. One may offer an attractive promotion where you have little competition on these products in your market . . . or the promotion would be too speculative for you. It's hard to say how much potential business is really out there in these products. You might promote them and see only a minimal increase in sales, temporarily or residually. Too risky. You haven't the cash for speculative ventures right now. You're in crisis mode.

REPOSITIONING OF BRANCH INVENTORIES

If you're a multi-branch distributor, the time of crisis offers a golden opportunity (and maybe an excuse) for some stringent repositioning of stocks around the branch network. In normal times, the branch managers and their salesmen would scream and throw tantrums if you tried these steps . . . but when you tell them: "We *must* do this! The company is in a crisis!" . . . well, they react differently. The tantrums are shorter.

You should have classified all stock items in all branches as Class 1 through Class 13. (If you're unfamiliar with this, again read "Distribution Inventory Management for the 1990's!"). Class 1's are the faster-moving products; Class 13 are the dogs. Classification is done independently, branch by branch. The same item could be a Class 1 in Dallas . . . a Class 11 in Oklahoma City. It sells very well in one branch but moves much more slowly in the other.

You can guess what you should do . . . even in normal times, but certainly here in the crisis period: Move all the stock from Oklahoma City to Dallas. Dallas doesn't have to reorder from the supplier next time. If Oklahoma City does sell one, they transfer it back or Dallas ships directly to the Oklahoma customer. Depending on how serious the crisis, move up the Classes as far as you need to. Begin by repositioning all Class 13, 12, and 11 items to other branches where they're in classes 1 through 4. If that's not enough to generate the cash needed, move on up into Classes 10, 9, and 8.

Yes, there'll be a negative result in the branches from which the stock was taken . . . but which items are affected? Only the slower-moving, those ordered infrequently by customers in those markets. When they order next time, there'll be a one-day delay in getting the merchandise to them. Bread and butter items are unaffected. They're still available locally in each branch.

Remember, the company may be fighting for its very life. You can't keep right on operating exactly the same way as before. **Something's** got to change! Sacrifices have to be made. Salesmen have to get into the fight too. They have to use every professional selling skill to keep customers satisfied even when everything's not on the local branch shelves in unlimited quantity as it was before . . . but you'll see a significant overall company inventory decrease by moving the slow products to places where they'll sell sooner, and the actual risk to sales is minimized.

SELECTIVELY REDUCE SAFETY ALLOWANCES

Finally, there's one other step you can take. It's discussed last because you should do all the other things first. This one involves the most risk, and has the greatest potential to backfire on you if not performed very carefully. On many stock items, you can reduce the amount of safety stock built in to your inventory by the normal replenishment-timing controls.

Remember from the last chapter, I suggest a 50% safety allowance factor in a stock item's order point to begin with. It may have to be increased later on, but 50% is a good starting point. A typical order point might look like this:

(Usage Rate × Lead Time) + 50% Safety Allowance = OP

(100   × 1 Month) +   50   = 150

The 50 units of stock in the safety allowance is there to protect you from variations in the usage rate during the lead time or in the lead time itself. It's there to keep you from running out of stock. It triggers the replenishment ordering process early enough to prevent a stockout on the item.

There are a few items in almost any inventory, however, that really don't need a 50% safety allowance. There aren't many, but there are some. Ordinarily, I wouldn't advise you to try to find them. It's safer to operate with a little more "pad" in the order point than not enough, so these few items' inventory excesses aren't worth the risk or trouble to find and remove them . . . but as said earlier, these are not normal times. Exceptional steps are needed.

Which Items Are Candidates for Less Safety?

Most distributors have some items carried in stock with relatively steady sales and very reliable suppliers. The suppliers delivers like clockwork and have for years. Customers buy these items in the same fashion. Sales over the past six months might be: 96, 110, 88, 115, 104, and 87. Yes, I **know** you don't have many like this, but every distributor has some! You could reduce the safety allowance to 25% . . . in the example above, cut it to 25 units instead of 50 . . . and do very well. Sales are steady and predictable; the supplier is reliable. You don't need as much "variation" protection on this item.

If you stock 10,000 items in total, there may be 500 in this category. Find them and reduce the safety stock. The inventory impact can be significant. If, however, you try . . . and can identify only 2 out of the first 200 items considered, then forget this! It won't impact the inventory size enough to justify the risk to customer service.

SUMMARY

There you have 'em . . . a few ideas to try when inventories *must* come down for one reason or another. There's no choice. Company survival may depend on the cash generated by the reduction. Please keep in mind: These are not normal modes of operation. Only the repositioning of branch stocks is a step that should be part of your day-to-day inventory lifestyle. Each of the others represents either risk to customer service or risk of personnel burnout and turnover. Use these tactics only when the wolf really *is* at the door . . . not to offset mountains of dead stock you've been too lazy to attack or rampant purchasing SWAG that's overloaded the warehouse.

Hidden Problems: Posting, Costing, and Administration 12

If you're the President, you may scan this chapter quickly and feel that you can just move on ahead. It labors through more details. If you're the Purchasing Manager, or a Data Processing Manager responsible to program an effective system, you'd better read very closely. You can't skip on by. The conditions discussed here can cause serious grief if handled badly . . . and even you, Mr. or Ms. President, need to work your way carefully through these topics if you're now searching the market for new software. Should you sign-on with a package that bungles the processes of this chapter, it'll cost you dearly. All manner of "hidden" problems will damage your profits.

The Non-Thinking Computer

These problems are not as obvious as many others, because computers are pretty dumb. They don't warn you when you've overlooked something critical in their programming. True, they're blazingly fast in assimilating massive quantities of information, crunching it 96 different ways, and giving it back to you wrapped however you wish . . . but they just don't think. If you fail to program the right steps when a weird condition is encountered, the machine may sidestep it completely and continue on down the normal path. Or it hits a fork in the road and takes the wrong fork. The most obvious choice (to a person) isn't obvious at all to the machine.

No warnings. No sirens. Misleading data is created or lousy productivity evolves, but like an unpainful (at first) cancer, you can't detect what's really happening to you. When you finally do feel pain, you may blame your people rather than the computer. Corrective action is also misdirected. So let's look at some of these choices and not-every-day conditions to keep these potentially hidden problems from making you sick.

POSTING THE HISTORY AFTER SUBSTITUTIONS

A customer calls: "Say, I'm in trouble. I need 50 of your item SKF 6203-2RS as quick as you can get 'em out here!" The item requested is very popular and customers often order it by brand name. Your inside salesperson replies: "Gosh, Jack, we're temporarily out of those right now. Got some due in early next week . . . but could you use a FAG 6203-2RS? I know you don't usually accept foreign products, but we guarantee the quality on the FAG and the price is a little better." The customer grumbles a bit, but then says OK.

Tell the Customer Clearly What You Did

When the sales order is keyed in, the system permits a special code for this line item to indicate that a substitute took place. The picking ticket and subsequent invoice show:

Ordered 50 SKF 6203-2RS

Shipped 50 FAG 6203-2RS

First, of course, you don't want some dodo on the customer's receiving dock to reject the shipment because your delivery document shows an item that doesn't match his purchase order copy. The guy who called may not have changed his P.O. paperwork, since the items are identical. The person in Receiving is new to the company and to the industry. He doesn't know yet that the two items are the same . . . and he's trying super-hard to do a careful job.

Remember this principle *anytime* a substitution is made on an order for any reason. Always show the item as originally ordered or requested . . . and the item actually shipped. You'll avoid unnecessary confusion and maybe some very costly steps to straighten out the mess. Imagine the trouble for your customer if his Receiving crew does send the item back with your driver. You'll now have to spend expensive effort to get the item back out there quickly. You don't want problems with their Accounts Payable people either: "This isn't the item we ordered. We're not paying this invoice!" Productivity is a key . . . remember? If your employees have to spend a lot of time on this kind of baloney, when it could have been avoided by one small entry on the invoice, you're wasting their work-hours.

Posting the Usage History

Now the critical point: Which of the two items gets the usage recorded in history? The item **requested** . . . *not* the one you shipped. If both are solid stock items, you want the computer to build up inventory based on what the customer wanted. In our example, the SKF 6203-2RS gets 50 units posted in the usage history. The FAG 6203-2RS has the balance reduced, of course, but shows nothing in history for this transaction. Otherwise the computer takes off down the wrong path at the end of the month when calculating usage rates and new ordering controls. Here would be incorrect computer logic:

> "Boy, your usage on that FAG 6203-2RS is beginning to pick up. I'd better suggest more inventory. The usage on the SKF item seems to have fallen off. Guess I'd better recommend less stock on that one."

Is this tricky to program and execute? A little . . . but worth the effort. The hardest part may be getting salesmen to record on the order what the customer wanted . . . and then a special code for that line item showing the substitute.

Automatic Substitutions

Some distributors carry numerous "generic" products, where most customers couldn't care less which brand is delivered . . . but where a few customers do have brand preferences. For the customers who aren't picky, the computer can be programmed to substitute automatically from the first available brand when a specified part number can't be provided. Although not nearly as critical in this situation, it's still basically a good idea to post usage to the item as requested . . . even when the computer does the substituting. The salesmen need not do any coding up front. When the computer subs, it knows it did so and can print all documents and post usages correctly.

Substituting on the Back-End as Well as the Front

While on the subject of automatic subs, consider this scene: A customer tells you when ordering:

> "Listen, I need an unmounted bearing like an SKF 6203-2RS very badly. I'll take any brand you have." Trouble is . . . you don't have anything available in any brand right now. Purchase orders are due in from three different suppliers very soon, but nothing's here today. The system would have subbed automatically had any other brand been in stock.

> The customer allows his request to be placed on backorder, and the part number recorded is SKF 6203-2RS. In comes a shipment of FAG 6203-2RS. What happens? In most software, nothing. The system doesn't sub on the back-end as well as the front. The customer's backorder continues to wait for the SKF material to arrive.

> You can imagine what the customer says when he calls a few days later to check on his order: "You mean you've had a perfectly acceptable item in stock for over a week and you haven't yet shipped my order? Jerk, I *told* you I didn't care what brand I got. What's the matter with your company? Don't you want my business?"

Good software "remembers," in effect, that the customer approved a sub and executes accordingly at the receiving end also. The computer says to itself:

> "Hmmm . . . just got in a bunch of FAG 6203-2RS. Do I have in my records any waiting backorders for this item? If so, fill them. Now, do

I have any waiting backorders for a directly-interchangeable item? Did the customer say in his file or by code on this order that a sub was OK? Fill all backorders in that category also."

Productivity . . . Always the Objective

Distributors often have to assign a person to double-check the customer backorder file manually ever so often, to avoid this kind of embarrassment. Agnes has to check each backorder weekly to see if it can now be filled from some other brand. What does that cost? How long will they survive if required to "manhandle" situations like this all through the order-processing steps . . . when the computer should have taken care of them? You're beginning to see, I hope, why the software you select is critical to your survival in the 21st century.

REBATES

Here's another tricky problem to be sure your system handles correctly: Rebates from suppliers. In a very competitive situation with a customer, you realize that you'd have to sell at your cost or below to get the business. You relay that information to your supplier who says:

> "Listen . . . I *want* our products in that customer! Go out there and quote a price that gets the contract. Each month, just provide proof that you sold the items and quantities, and I'll rebate the difference between your actual cost and selling price to give you a 20% profit."

The distributor has at least three problems in such a deal:

A. Potential costing steps that lead to massive adjustments later
B. Potential for very disgruntled salesmen
C. Potential for extensive (and expensive) administrative work

First . . . the Costing Problem

The distributor usually brings the contract items into stock at normal prices from the supplier. For example, the vendor's invoice

shows a cost of $1.00 for one of the items under the rebate arrange-
ment. That's the regular cost. That's the cost at which a receipt of
1,000 goes into inventory initially. $1,000 is added to the book
inventory. We pay the supplier $1,000.

During the first month of the new contract, 500 of this item are
delivered out to the customer at a selling price of $1.00 each. No
problem . . . we *knew* we'd have to sell 'em at that price, which of
course shows zero gross profit. We'll get money back from the
supplier later. $500 comes out of inventory; the cost of goods sold
is $500; gross profit is zero. 10 separate deliveries were needed to
get the full 500 to the customer . . . just as he requested them.
Are we headed for a problem? Almost certainly. This isn't the best
way to handle a rebate sale. There are several hidden problems in
this approach.

Salesmen Are Bent Out of Shape

Since no gross profit is shown, no sales commission is paid at the
end of this current period. Later when the supplier pays up, we'll
go back and figure out what the true gross profits were, calculate
the commissions, and add the money to a salesman's check. The
supplier's a bit slow processing the rebate credits . . . and on the
average, two months elapse before the salesman sees his money.
Here's what he says:

> "Here we go again. The company always seems to find some way to
> stick it to me. How in the world can I tell *now* whether or not they got
> my commissions right on sales from two months ago? This whole deal
> stinks. I'm better off selling stuff the regular way. Then at least I have
> some way of checking commissions earned against what I see in each
> month's check. From now on, I won't fool with any more of these
> dumb rebate deals."

Salesmen are sensitive, and rightfully so, about their paychecks.
They think they should be paid promptly and accurately after all the
work poured into making a sale. If an administrative procedure
slows down the paycheck or casts a cloud of doubt on the accuracy,
the salesmen may begin to take compensating action.

After the Rebate: Massive Manipulation of Records

Finally the supplier issues $100 as a rebate on the 500 units sold two months ago. Remember, we're entitled to a 20% profit on the $1.00 sale of each of the 500. Now . . . two months later . . . we must dig back out of the computer records each individual line on each order where the rebate sale was made. Each line gets an adjustment of .20 per item delivered to cost of goods sold and to gross margin. Commissions are now figured and paid. Of course, since we've gone across two month-ends since then, journal entries for the total amounts must be made long after the fact to gross margin, cost of goods sold, and commission numbers for the month of the sales. What a mess!

A Better Approach: Use Post-Rebate Numbers

A less-troublesome approach is to cost each rebate-sale line item on the sales orders at the *post-rebate values* . . . right from the outset. The sale up above that goes out for a $1.00 price is costed right off at 80 cents each. At the very start, each transaction has the cost of goods sold and the gross margin recorded as they'll finally wind up after the supplier sends the rebate. Sales commissions may be paid at the end of the month . . . and they too are correct. The salesmen are satisfied.

True, until you get the rebate, you've understated the inventory value that's actually gone out the door . . . considering how much was paid for the stuff . . . and gross margin, likewise, has been overstated by the same amount. The advantage, however, is that each transaction is valued already as it will ultimately need to be. None will have to be adjusted two months from now when the rebate is actually credited by the supplier. All month-end statements and reports are clean. None will have to be modified later.

When the rebate is received, two journal entries clean up the shortage and overage: Taking more dollars from inventory and adding to income by the rebate amount. These entries are made to totals . . . not to individual sales order transactions. Those are already correct.

Reduce the Administrative Load

It's burdensome to track rebate transactions manually all through the month, make the appropriate document copies, develop the summaries and send an official report to the supplier . . . in order to prove the sales and get the rebate. What if several suppliers are involved, 15 customers and 456 items? Poor Agnes, or somebody (maybe a team), faces a mountain of work right after month-end close, and some amount of clerical work is necessary every day.

A good computerized system builds all the rebate information right into the regular pricing files. When a customer's been quoted a "rebatable" price, it's recorded in the pricing file for that item, customer, and supplier. When he orders, the computer has a little talk with itself:

> "Well look at this: Ol' ABC Industries is ordering a FAF 203PP. That's under a rebate deal for him. His price is $1.00. I've been given special programming for this. I'm supposed to cost out the sale at 80 cents. That's what I'll do.
>
> Next, they told me to keep track of all rebate sales by item and customer for the month. When the month ends, I'm to prepare a special report for Agnes with a listing by supplier of all rebate activity, the totals, and rebate amounts due.
>
> All through the month, with the new 'Imaging' capability I now have, they've been feeding me copies of every sales order delivery receipt where a rebate was involved. Keep these in case they need copies later to document the summary report I've provided for the supplier."

You can see what happens. All through the month, the computer prices, costs, and tracks all rebate-sale activity. At month-end, a report goes to one person . . . who sends the appropriate listing to each supplier in summary form as a rebate request. If a supplier demands to see actual sales documents, they're available very quickly but otherwise are not printed. Further programming follows up each request after 30 days if not yet received, so that rebates credits or payments are made on time.

Rebating has become ever more popular as the competitive picture tightens and recessions come and go. Good software performing as outlined here saves many hours of administrative "manhandling," lightens the transaction-adjustment requirements, and keeps your sales force happy when rebates are an important selling tool. If you're to have the productivity necessary for a "quality" operation, ask about such capabilities during the next software demo.

LET THE COMPUTER REMOVE RECORDS OF LOST BUSINESS

Let's say that one of your top-rated salesmen walks in with some bad news:

> "Boss, I've just been out to ABC Industries to follow up on our bid for next year's contract. We didn't get it. They told me that Ajax Distribution over in Fort Worth underbid us this time."

Some "lost sale" conversation is just that . . . conversation . . . but this news represents business you **know** you won't get next year. You'd better make some adjustments if you expect the computerized system to suggest proper replenishment controls next year. The computer, as things stands right now, has month-by-month usage histories for all stock items going back for a year . . . and that history includes the ABC Industries usage. For some items under the contract, ABC accounted for 45% of the total sales.

A Perfect Computer Exercise

Program your computer to go back through last year's records of sales by item by customer and identify the items ABC bought, in which months, and in what quantity. Now have the computer go back to each of the months and create an "Override" history entry with the ABC activity removed, like this:

Item SKF 32B	Jan	Feb	Mar	Apr	May	Jun	Jul	Aug	Sep	Oct	Nov	Dec
Actual Usage	110	75	40	190	27	95	128	12	146	58	91	116
ABC's Sales	−61	−25		−100			−80		−100		−15	−70
Override Usage History	49	50		90			48		46		76	46

Next year, the computer forecasts usage from this history:

	Jan	Feb	Mar	Apr	May	Jun	Jul	Aug	Sep	Oct	Nov	Dec
	49	50	40	90	27	95	48	12	46	58	76	46

You'll recall from my earlier book that I want a buyer to have the capability to override an item's history for any given month . . . replacing the actual usage picture with an "override" for forecasting purposes. He or she does that, for example, with unusually high but non-recurring sales or when a stockout lasts too long on an item. Here's another of these overrides, but this one's done by the computer after (what could be) an extensive data search, calculation, and file-adjustment exercise.

ABC's sales are removed from history . . . not from the records of what actually occurred . . . but from those history fields the computer will use next year to recommend inventory levels. It could be a massive job. No one would have attempted it manually. If the adjustments aren't made, however, you run the risk of building inventories next year anticipating sales that have gone elsewhere. Again . . . look for software that can perform steps like this for you: Reduce the clerical load but still make the adjustments so vital to profitable asset management.

WHAT ABOUT OTHER LOST SALES?

I'm skeptical about most lost-sale statements. The salesmen, of course, would like purchasing people to respond to every one and build up the stock with all manner of overrides. Consider this little scene:

A customer calls looking for 50 of a stock item that you happen to be out of right now. Your salesman tells him: "Sorry Frank, we're out of that, but I've got a shipment due in next Tuesday."

The customer replies: "Gosh, that's too bad. I can't wait that long. I'll find them somewhere else." If this is reported as a lost sale, the buyer might be expected to make usage-history or control overrides to allow for the 50 units that slipped away.

Better wait on that. The customer calls back on Tuesday, gets a different telephone salesman: "Hey, did you get in those SKF 6203-2RS from your supplier yet?" The salesman answers: "Yes, they just came in this morning." Customer: "Great, send me 50 on tomorrow morning's truck!"

What happened here? One of two things:

1. The customer looked around town and couldn't find any, or . . .

2. He was irritated when he first called that you couldn't take care of his need immediately. He realized that he'd have to call back again later to get the order placed. That hacked him off, and he expressed the irritation . . . but he had no intention of going elsewhere for the item.

If you make an inventory-level adjustment based on the 50 units you thought you'd lost, and then the computer reacts normally to the 50 units sold on Tuesday . . . what happens to inventory size on the item? It's too high. What's the Number 1 cause of distributor bankruptcy today? . . . loss of sales? No, that's Number 7. Number 1 is mismanaged assets, with inventory being the largest asset. I've pounded this into your "memory banks" over and over throughout this book, because every distributor *must* get that message if they expect to be a business entity in the 21st century. There are many reasons why an inventory climbs beyond acceptable limits. Overreacting to lost sale "conversation" is one of them.

A Customer Searching for an Item

Then there's the customer who calls one day and asks:

"Listen, do you guys stock an SKF 82X?" Your salesmen replies: "No, we don't carry that. I could order some for you, but it'll take about

three weeks from the supplier. Will you be needing the 82X often?"
The customer: "Boy, we sure will! I was hoping you'd have that in
stock. We'll be using a lot of 'em over the next year."

Your salesman walks in to the Sales Manager's office:

> "Boss, I'm getting a lot of requests for the SKF 82X (there's been only
> the one, but heck there *may be* more). I think we ought to add it
> to stock."

What happens if you do add it to stock? Well . . . that customer's
going to call six other distributors in your area with the same story.
If all seven of you add it to stock, what happens to six distributors?
Yeah, they wind up with dead stock. The customer intends to buy
regularly from only one source, the guy with the cheapest price.
Hopefully, that wouldn't be you.

Make Adjustments Only When You're Certain

Yes, I know that some "lost sales" really are. My caution here is to
make very certain before adjusting inventory levels. If you *know* the
business went elsewhere . . . but likely will return to you if you do
a better job of maintaining stock . . . then OK, make the adjustment to compensate for sales the computer never recorded. But
don't overlook the fact that occasionally the lost sales are perma-
nent, even when you *are* sure. The customer who you failed to
service **will not** be back to you for that item. For all these reasons,
you should be hesitant to just plop more stock into the system when
a salesman complains of lost business.

SUMMARY

Substitutions, Backorders, Rebates, Lost Sales . . . real and
imagined . . . naggy problems that are often overlooked when
software is first designed. Yet each has an impact on inventory.
Handled well, inventory is kept down but service still remains at
high levels. Administrative costs are reduced and productivity per

employee is high. Handled poorly, the inventory climbs. Productivity is lousy, and your new owners have a real mess to straighten out when they take over. True, these functions alone might not cause you to become a non-profit organization. If, however, you take on software that can't perform well here . . . it's a good bet that the package performs poorly in other critical asset-management areas also.

A New Attitude Toward New Stock Items

13

There's a dusty old saying that every salesman learns in the first grade:

"You can't sell out of an empty wagon!"

I'm not sure why elementary teachers isolate all future salesmen for this special training, but they do. No one else hears it. The teachers use visual aids like small red wagons, which are pulled around the classroom (empty) at early-morning sessions when only the future salesmen are present. The little salespeople of the future don't pay much attention to arithmetic or geography, but they latch on to this teaching. They remember. They quote it often all the rest of their lives. It becomes sort of a "life motto." However, there's another statement that, for some reason, is omitted from the salesman's educational background:

"It's important to sell what's on the wagon!"

Adding New Items to Stock . . . Always Necessary

Don't misunderstand my teasing here. I *know* that it's vital for every distributor to add fresh new items to the stock list regularly.

It's just that past practices for many companies in this area were pretty haphazard. Items found their way onto the shelves for too many reasons, authorized by too many people without accountability, and the results were damaging. They developed massive inventories, much of which was dead or slow-moving.

Let's now discuss this new-stock decision with a view to improving the odds that a new item will sell. Recognize that changes in attitude are necessary. If you're to improve your performance on new items, you can't keep adding them under the same logic you used in 1985 or even 1990. Of course, changing an attitude is the toughest assignment you can draw. People don't like to change. If not managed carefully, they'll drift very quickly right back into old patterns and habits . . . no matter how rigid you think your new rules are.

Controlling Who Can Authorize a Stock Item

Begin by taking a bold step: Assign full authority for approval in just one person when an item is first stocked *anywhere* in the company. Example: Somebody out in the Keokuk branch is requesting that six new items be added to stock in the Ajax Manufacturing line of differential diaphramalators. This line of products is brand new to the company. No one else anywhere stocks these items. Keokuk may not add these six items until approval is granted by the person given this authority. Why? Someone a little more objective than Keokuk needs to check out several other alternatives:

1. If the company has several branch locations, there may already be a line of similar products stocked somewhere else. Why not require Keokuk to transfer-in this product line for their needs until actual sales patterns develop, rather than adding a duplicate line right now? At least, consider that option.

2. If the line is approved for stock, it's important that the part numbers, descriptions, units of measure, and sequence for computer display and/or printing be established in a manner consistent with all other items now in the file. You don't want Keokuk personnel to create this data for the very first time. Who knows how they'll enter the numbers and

descriptions, especially if they're inexperienced or in a hurry to get the job done so that a purchase order can be placed? They may also omit certain vital data, intending to add it later.

3. Each new stock item should begin its life with estimates or assignments already in the file to assure it begins under solid control: What sales per month are expected? What Lead Time? What's the opening Order Point and Order Quantity? Where in the warehouse do you plan to put it on arrival? What's the expected unit cost? Who's the Buyer assigned to this item? What's the initial Review Cycle for the product line?

There are excellent reasons for this set of requirements. True, you can't put a new stock item onto the shelves in quite the "fast and loose" fashion of the past, but the requirements bring some definite benefits.

The Need to Slow-Down a Bit and Be Sure

Although the approval process is swift when all required data is provided, it does require anyone wanting to add an item or product group to do some homework. The research just might cause a branch manager, for example, to rethink the request, especially when a salesman can't come up with anything more than: "Boss, I really think we need to stock this."

The Need for Complete Information

It's also important that every new stock item begin its life with complete information in the files. How many times have you put something into stock only to discover six months later that it carried an incomplete description . . . or it *still* doesn't have a good unit cost recorded . . . or you can't find it in the warehouse because it still has no location shown? Maybe you ran out of stock because no one had yet entered an Order Point. Oh . . . they **intended** to put all this stuff in the computer records sooner or later, but in the rush to get the item ordered initially from the supplier . . . well, it just didn't get in there.

Another Lesson from Your Bank

Isn't this the real picture? You're about to add dollar bills to the shelves. Remember in an early chapter, I talked about this new attitude of seeing the inventory as if it were negotiable currency. It makes sense to set up a "new account" with all necessary information to be sure you can find the money, that you know what it looks like, that you replenish properly when you run low, and that you can keep accurate records of how much is there. Picture this little scene:

> You walk into a bank where you want to open a checking account. The receptionist says: "Take a seat right over there, please, and the young lady will be with you in a minute to get all the information we'll need about you and your new account."

> You reply: "I haven't got time for this! I'm in a big hurry. I'm not going to waste all this time giving you that information. I found some of your blank drafts over on that table, and I'm going to write checks this afternoon on this bank!"

> The receptionist says: "Go ahead . . . we'll just trash each one when it comes in. None will be honored. We'd have no control. We must have the necessary start-up information."

Do you see the point? A "new account" requires quite a bit of detailed up-front information if the bank is to handle all transactions smoothly. A new stock item needs that same kind of up-front information, but distributors are often in such a big hurry to get the stuff in the door that they open the account without critical data.

THE NEED FOR COMMITMENT

In this section, I'll re-hash counsel from "Distribution Inventory Management For The 1990's" but with more emphasis or emotion perhaps. A need for "commitment" from somebody, before new stock goes onto the shelves, is critical . . . even more so now than when that earlier book came out. The days are gone when distributors added new stock on a speculative basis: "Gosh, I sure hope this stuff sells" . . . or "Hmmm . . . that new product line seems promising. Let's put in a full array and see how it goes."

When it didn't "go," the cost was high and no one could be held accountable. Customers hadn't committed to buy nor salesmen to sell the new inventory. "Hey, it's not *my* fault!" . . . said a salesman. "I never said that I could sell those new products." Today, and certainly in the 21st century, distributors must adopt a completely new attitude about commitments: Get one from *somebody* or don't add the new stock! It comes from the customer, the Sales Manager, or an individual salesman.

A Commitment from the Customer

A scene from your past. Harry over at ABC Industries calls one morning:

> "Say . . . I need you guys to add six new items to your stock for my exclusive use. OK, I **know** they're a little bit weird, and can't be returned to your supplier. I know they have long lead times, but if you'll add these six items for us, you'll get all our business on them next year. Not only that . . . we try to help distributors who work with us like this. There'll be substantial additional volume on other items that we haven't bought from you before. Of course right now, I can't promise anything precisely on what that extra purchase volume will total."

If this was a good customer, how quickly did you have the requested items on your shelves for ol' Harry? Pretty quick. The lead time passed and the merchandise was sitting in the warehouse awaiting orders from ABC. Now a nagging question: "What's the Number 1 cause of distributor failure today?" Wonderful . . . you're catching on! And how did you get a lot of that non-moving merchandise in the first place? Wasn't it verbal deals you made with customers just like this one, where good ol' "Harry" didn't come through?

Times have changed. Today, you need a written commitment from Harry. Ask for a blanket order with release dates and quantities. Ask for a blanket order with an end-date to the arrangement, at which all inventory you still have can be shipped and invoiced. Ask

for a letter Harry signs, on his company letterhead, in which he
spells out how he intends to buy this special stock. Get it in writing.
No more verbal deals.

You Want a Psychological Advantage

Don't misunderstand the intent here. I'm not suggesting that you
file away some document that you'll try to enforce later. You don't
want this written agreement to enforce it. You want it to gain a
huge psychological advantage over the other three distributors
. . . your competitors . . . in the region with whom Harry made
exactly the same deal. You didn't think he'd do such a thing? It
seems doggone unethical.

Well, remember the kind of items he's asked you to stock.
They're not the norm. They're hard to get, have a long lead time,
and would have to be considered unusual. Harry isn't 100% positive what his requirements will be next year on these six squirrels
. . . so what's he done? He's set up four "pockets" of stock around
the region to be sure he'll have no possible supply problem. His
needs could triple the expected levels and he'll be OK. If you have a
written agreement of any type, and your three competitors have
only verbal "handshake" deals . . . .who receives *all* of Harry's
business next year on these six items? You do. What do your competitors get? Two things: Excuses and Dead Stock. Harry isn't sure
exactly what your legal rights are or how far you might push them,
but he knows precisely what the legal rights of the other three guys
are. Zero. He gives you any orders he has.

Any Attempt to Enforce the Deal
Drives Off the Customer

No matter how seemingly ironclad your written agreement with
Harry, it's not wise to actually try to hold him to it. Let's say that
Harry gave you a letter stating:

"ABC Industries asks you to stock the following six items for our
exclusive use. ABC guarantees to buy at least 10 of each item each

month. Should you have any inventory of these products remaining on December 31, you may ship and invoice it all to ABC. We will then pay under 30 day terms."

Looks pretty good, doesn't it? You're perfectly protected, right? **WRONG!** December 31st rolls around, and you call Harry:

"Harry, it's time to wind up our special-stock arrangement that we began last January. It must have been an unexpected year for you there at ABC Industries. You didn't purchase as much as you specified . . . and in accord with the letter you signed, I'm shipping today all remaining stock we have on those six items."

What does Harry say?

"Gosh . . . don't do *that!* Don't even think about it. You're right. Things haven't gone at all as we'd anticipated. We're expecting activity to really pick up next year, so here's what I'll do: I'll mail over another letter with a new December 31 end-date. We'll just rollover this deal one more year. You'll still have a guarantee on the stock, but we'll have another year to use it up."

Your answer:

"No way, Harry. I'm going to enforce the letter I have now!"

Harry has one last word for you:

"I wouldn't advise that you do that. If you ship that stock, we may or may not pay for it by next August . . . and you'll never see another order of any kind from ABC Industries."

You don't want the written agreement to enforce it. You want it for the psychological edge it gives you over everybody else in town with whom ABC made the same special-stock deal.

A Commitment from Your Salesman

There are times when it's impossible to get anything in writing from the customer. Yet the customer is a good one, and his request for special stock can't be dismissed just because he won't sign anything formal. Your salesman, Harold, walks in one afternoon:

> "Boss, I've just been out at ABC Industries talking to ol' Harry, and you'll recall he wants us to add six special stock items just for him. Well I know you said you wanted something in writing on deals like this, but Harry won't do that. He works on a handshake only. A verbal agreement is the best he'll do. He also told me that if we won't stock this stuff, he'd find someone else to do it and then we could expect a dramatic drop in our overall business from him next year.
>
> Boss, you know he's been a good account, and I've been bustin' my clavicle to build up the business at ABC. Are you going to support me in this or not?"

Your reply:

> "No problem, Harold. Just fill in this blank form I've got here and sign it. Here are spaces for the six items we'll be adding, and that column there is where you write down the number of units you commit to sell to ABC each month on each item. ..oh, and before you sign at the bottom, note that last paragraph. If any of the initial stock that we add for ABC under this arrangement is still here after six months . . . and we can't return it to our supplier . . . then at that point, *you* and the company split the 30% per year carrying cost."

Harold may refuse to sign such a commitment. If he does, *NO INVENTORY* is added for his customer. What's the Number 1 cause of distributor bankruptcy today . . . lack of sales? How about "Too Much Inventory"? How'd you get all that merchandise that's now sitting in the warehouse gathering dust? Didn't it result from this kind of stuff? Some salesman said: "Boy, they're **REALLY** going to be ordering a lot of this new material!!" When it didn't turn out that way, the salesman said: "Hmmm . . . too bad. I guess I was wrong." And he walked away. The company took the hit. The salesman left on vacation.

Those days are gone. In this economic climate, there must be a formal commitment from **somebody** . . . customer, salesman, or perhaps the sales manager . . . before more dollars are placed out on the warehouse shelves. You simply cannot speculate with inventory any longer.

Again, Harold's Commitment Has a Psychological Impact

When you boil down what Harold signed, the impact in most cases is more psychological than financial. Harold's at risk *only* on the initial stock brought in to support the agreement. If ABC Industries lives up to their end of the bargain long enough that stock must be replenished on one or all the items . . . Harold's off the hook on any replenishment stock. The company takes the full risk on that. Harold has part ownership, so to speak, only on the *initial* stock that's brought in.

Let's say also that $1,000 of new inventory is involved. The worst of Harold's nightmares occurs: ABC fails to buy one piece of anything. After six months, the full $1,000 still waits out in the warehouse. Now the 30% per year carrying cost kicks in . . . $300 per year. Harold's share is $150 per year. It's charged to him monthly. Harold must pay $12.50 per month. It's not a big deal, unless of course a lot of inventory value is involved . . . but this charge does get Harold's attention. He's walking around the warehouse one day (not a good idea for him to be out there, but he is anyway), and he sees the dusty stock sitting there for ABC Industries. He thinks to himself:

> "Hey, the time's about up on that stuff. I'm going to go call ol' Harry and see why he's not buying this material like he said he would. If he doesn't take it, I'd better get on a campaign to find some other home for this stock at some price. I sure don't want this inventory to be part of my Christmas bonus."

That's right, Harold. You have a vested interest in this stock. You'll do well to use every professional skill you have to move it out . . . and more importantly, think very carefully before asking the company to add new material in the first place. You'd better be very confident that the customer will indeed buy it as he has promised.

THE "ADD-ONE/DROP-ONE" RULE

When the Sales Manager or a Product Manager wants to add a large group of items . . . 200 in a new product line or 50 in a new category . . . you still need to follow the earlier suggestions of getting expected usage data on each item. Another effective policy is to then say to the Sales Manager:

> "Frank, it's important for us to continually 'prune' our stock item list. As we add these 50 new items, you must identify 50 old items that we can drop. Find 50 that we can now categorize: 'Do Not Reorder For Stock'. We'll use up the inventory and then not replenish them.
>
> The items to drop need not be equivalent in value or type to those you're adding. You may want to add 50 new motors; you can identify 50 seals to drop . . . or a mixture of item types. It doesn't matter. We just want 50 for 50. 50 added . . . 50 dropped."

Can the Sales Manager rather easily find 50 candidates to drop? Sure. What does he or she want more than anything else right now? To add those 50 new stock items. He's chomping at the bit to get them in the warehouse and unleash his sales force on 'em. He'll identify 50 dusty ones that aren't that vital to the overall sales program. The key point: *Sales people are the ones making the drop-from-stock decision.* They can't come back later and gripe about one of the discontinued 50 not being on the shelf.

WHICH BRANCHES CARRY THE NEW STOCK ITEM OR LINE?

Often when a new product line is approved by the company, every one of the 10 branches is allowed to bring in a "representative" stock array. Each branch manager thinks that his sales will really take off. Usually that doesn't happen. Two of the branches show good activity on the new stuff within 60 days, but the other eight locations are much slower getting under way. Worse . . . three branches show no substantial sales after a year.

Since this is nearly always the pattern on new products, wouldn't it make sense to start a little more cautiously with the initial investment of inventory dollars? The home office location begins with the full approved array of products. They act as a central distribution point for many of the branches. Most sales are shipped from the central warehouse directly to the outlying customers, until a clearer picture of volume develops. The larger branches are given only those items for stock that promise the best chances for quick new volume. The smaller branches begin with no local inventory at all. Everything they sell ships within 24 hours from the central warehouse directly to their customers.

Yes . . . there's guesswork involved, and you'll make some mistakes. You must be ready to adjust quickly. Branches with heavy "walk-in" or counter trade need a wider range of the new products on their shelves right from the start . . . than does a branch that delivers or ships nearly everything. New products involve a high degree of pure SWAG. You're trying to figure out how often which customers will buy which items in what quantities, and there's little or no track record. The odds for bad guesses are pretty high. The odds are also high that you'll wind up with lots of new merchandise that doesn't sell at all or is stocked in the wrong branch. Start cautiously on new inventory but be ready to adjust quickly when sales patterns develop.

TIE THE MANAGER'S PAY TO INVENTORY SIZE

This counsel seems almost trite to offer. Yet, I still see too many distributors who allow managers to add huge inventory investments without any direct involvement of the manager's pay. The controller calls once in a while to gripe about how much inventory a particular branch carries . . . but other than that and the "will-o'-the-wisp" profit sharing plan at year-end (where no one understands the calculation), big inventories have no financial penalty. The solution: Tie each manager's pay directly to inventory size. When you decide to keep a big inventory on your shelves, Mr. or Ms. Manager, you'll feel the impact in your compensation. The mechanics for doing this vary of course, but one of the most effective is to charge each branch 2½% of their inventory-value per month back against operating expenses. That works out to 30% per year . . . the carrying cost. Pay each manager based on the operating profit of the branch.

A branch carrying $250,000 in inventory gets a $6,250 hit each month . . . $75,000 for the year . . . the carrying cost. If

annual sales ran $1 million with gross profit $220,000, that
$75,000 charge **really** cuts into the operating profit. Next year,
that manager finds a way to support the $1.1 million in sales from
only $100,000 in inventory. When a salesman says: "Boss, we
need to add item ABC 1432X to stock for my customer" . . . the
manager replies: "No John, I want you to go out there and try to
sell him the ABC 1433 which we already stock," or "If you sell the
1432X, we'll ship all orders directly from the central warehouse.
They carry that. We're not going to add it here." Maybe the decision is to pick up the 1432X from a competitor for those few times
this customer orders . . . and make only 10% gross margin. The
manager becomes very skilled in retaining the sales without
adding more local inventory. He or she has direct financial incentives to do so.

THE DUPLICATE PRODUCT LINE PROBLEM

The plague of many distributors are duplicate product lines. You
carry Black & Decker and also Skil. You have SKF bearings and also
Fafnir. Maybe it's Kohler and American Standard. Domestic products and the same things from overseas suppliers. Westinghouse
and G.E. products, etc. . . . you know the problem.

If I had a sure-fire formula for solving this headache, I'd already
be living in Kauai, Colorado, or somewhere. I wouldn't need
to write books, conduct seminars or mow the grass. I can offer
only counsel . . . but counsel based on many years of wrestling
with duplicate products and the excessive inventories that nearly
always result.

How Did You Get the Duplicates in the First Place?

Any attempt to solve this problem begins at the source. How did
the duplicate product lines evolve? Who made the decisions to
stock them and why? There's no single answer of course. Duplicate
lines are created for many reasons, some innocent and some not
so innocent:

1. You buy out or merge with another distributor who carries a competing line. Now you have both brands in the company. Before long the second line begins to show up in branches where you really don't want it. The branches are transferring material back and forth.

2. A major customer offers a systems contract with big volume, but his stipulation is for Brand B on a sizable group of items. You add it to stock in only one location and it's only for sale to him . . . .but like a virus, you've introduced the products into your company. Especially if some don't move as planned, you try to find other places to sell them, other branches. Now other customers are introduced to them and they like this new stuff. You haven't added sales volume. A portion simply transfers to Brand B, while many customers still prefer original Brand A.

3. A salesman with limited professional skills bends to minor pressure from a customer. You carry identical products, but to get an order your salesman agrees to special-order Brand B. Since the salesman committed the company, you must carry through. Unfortunately, each item on the order is for a quantity of six . . . while the minimum purchase from the supplier has to be 24 of each. Ten items are on the order. That salesman just created stock of 18 units on ten items in Brand B. Here you go again . . . the virus, etc.

4. You decide to take on a new product line to replace an old one. Everyone's excited. Trouble is . . . some customers (not many but a few important ones) object to the new line. They insist that you continue to supply them the old stuff. If you can still purchase the old line, you keep on buying material for the important accounts. Often the result is to spread the same level of sales across two product lines where before there was only one. Two inventories, however.

5. In the early days of your company, good product lines were hard to get (and keep). You'd take on a line when it was available . . . even though it wasn't your first choice . . . to be sure you had products in that category to sell. As sales grew, other lines were added but you were afraid to drop anything until the new supplier relationships matured. Once in a while a supplier took a line away. To try to keep everyone

happy, you spread your purchase volume across the duplicate lines. Ten years later, you're still doing that.

You could likely add several more scenarios under which duplicate products wind up on your shelves. Frankly, there's not much you can do about some of this other than to get tough after the fact and kill off as many items as you can by one of the other methods suggested in this chapter. The nature of the distribution business and how a company evolves over the years causes duplicate lines. For some of the scenes above, however . . . you *can* do something.

Watch What You Commit the Company to, Mr. or Ms. Salesperson

When a salesperson commits the company to do something for a customer, he or she at that moment puts your corporate integrity on the line. The customer forms an impression about your company based on how you perform. It doesn't matter that perhaps the salesman went beyond his authority. It doesn't matter that his simple: "No problem. We can do that for you!" may wind up costing the company a fortune. If you can back him up with perform-ance, and still stay in business, you should follow through . . . regardless of the cost. Your company's integrity is a precious, al-most priceless, commodity. Your "word" must mean something . . . regardless of whose mouth it comes from.

But there's another issue to be addressed: "You'd best be very careful Mr. or Ms. Salesperson. We'll do whatever you agree to. If you *do* exceed your authority . . . if the agreement stems from your ignorance, laziness, or professional sloppiness . . . you may very well get an opportunity to help pay for the mess. Here's an example:

> Louise . . . one of your salespeople . . . gets a request from a good customer to ship in 6 of an item you don't stock. She checks the supplier's catalog, finds the item, and notes the costs shown there. If the company buys only 6, our cost would be $5.60 each, and the customer might not like the $7.30 selling price. If we buy 36 at a time, however, our cost drops to $3.80 each. That would drop the selling price to $5.00. That's what Louise quotes for the 6.

When the sales order processes, Purchasing is alerted to the need for this non-stock item. The selling price is below our cost if only the six are purchased. When the buyer explains that to Louise, she replies: "Listen, that's the only way I could get that order! You must bring these items in at a cost which generates a reasonable gross profit." The buyer is cornered. Louise has committed the company to buy 36 . . . sell the 6 . . . and put the other 30 out in the warehouse somewhere. She just created a new stock item for you, even though she had no authority to do that.

Louise Receives an Instant Degree in Economics

You can almost guess what I'm about to say. The Buyer first checks with the Sales Manager for instructions as to how to proceed. One of two things should occur:

1. Only 6 are purchased. The $ 3.60 loss which the company takes on the sale (6 @ .60) is charged to Louise. It comes out of her commission this month.
2. 36 are purchased, but the cost of the 30 that wind up on the shelf ($150) is charged to Louise. The 30 stock units are placed into the inventory at no value. If Louise or anyone else ever sells them, 100% gross margin is reflected.

"You're saying, Graham, that the salesman should know how an item has to be bought before quoting a selling price! That's crazy." Is it? What's the Number 1 reason for distributor bankruptcy? How did you get all that strange inventory you now have in your warehouse? Wasn't it little scenes like this repeated over and over again, hundreds of times a year perhaps, across your 10 branches?

There should be very controlled procedures . . . very fast, but tightly controlled . . . whereby Louise can request stock-item-status for an item. Her manager reviews the request and either grants or denies it. If the item must remain non-stock, then Louise . . . again . . . checks with her manager *before quoting a price below the normal markup* you'd develop if purchasing buys only the quantity the customer wants.

Don't put us in a corner, Louise. Don't commit the company to something beyond your authority. If you do, we'll honor the commitment . . . but you'll bear the cost. Be sure to do your homework. Be sure you know how we'll have to buy the item before you quote the selling price. If you don't know, call the buyer first . . . right from the customer's office if necessary . . . but don't work from ignorance or laziness. If you do, and stock results that we don't want . . . you've bought it.

The New Supplier Takes All Your Old Stock

Some distributors can't pull off this next coup, but if you're a mid to large-sized company . . . this works very well. It depends also on how badly the new manufacturer wants you to take on his product line in place of the competitive line you now handle. You simply add this requirement to take on the line:

> The new manufacturer must take back all inventory of the old line as soon as his first shipment arrives in each branch location. He gives you credit on the basis of cost paid. He pays the freight to whatever designation he designates. The credit may be applied in payment of his first invoices . . . and it's done on a corporate basis. The total credit may be applied, regardless of how much material he shipped-in/took-back at any given location.

Now you find out how serious this supplier really is. Does he **really** want you to take on his line and drop the old one? Is all that conversation really valid about the value you'll add to his nation-wide distribution network? If he says: "Yes, I'm serious!," there's a way to prove it. Remove the old product line inventory as we begin. Help us avoid duplicate lines in any location. He recognizes, as you do, that sales on many of the old products will die very quickly after the new material arrives, but customer-acceptance on some of the new items may be slower than anticipated. He helps you absorb the "shock" of the product-line changeover.

SUMMARY

You may be thinking: "This is all too harsh. Graham is on some kind of crusade against the suppliers and our sales force. We'd never add any new stock items if we followed all the rigid rules of this chapter. Nobody would sell to us or want to work for us. Some customers wouldn't buy from us." Well, you'd better consider realistically the mourning period for each of these three groups if your company goes under:

A. Supplier: 17 Minutes   Time needed to find how much you owe him. He likely has already selected alternate distributors for your region . . . or can sign one quickly.

B. Salesman: 2 Days   1st day to play golf; 2nd to get a job with your competitor. He knows the products and if you're gone . . . controls some business.

C. Customer: 5 Days   Time to find a new source for 49er tickets, a new fishing lodge . . . and to find an open house some distributor has scheduled where he can drink free beer. He can buy all of your products from several other sources.

Take It Slow If You Must . . . But Get Moving

Maybe you can't adopt every concept right off the bat. Maybe you should ease into the tighter disciplines for adding new items. If you continue, however, with the "no-discipline" approach many distributors used in the past . . . you'd better start construction soon on a new, larger, much more expansive warehouse. You'll need it. Following that, locate a good bankruptcy lawyer. Why not locate first, if you can find them, the top executives from distributors who've failed in recent years. Some were industry leaders in their region just a few years back. Call and ask what counsel they'd offer about the failure to change attitudes on asset management. One former executive from a defunct Plumbing/Heating/AC company said this, in effect:

> "It took eleven years to build a sound business but only a few months to lose one. We relied too much on our history and failed to consider what was necessary for the future . . . and when we did begin to move, we had waited too long to get started. It's like a battleship. You

can turn the wheel but a change in direction isn't instantaneous. You don't see the results of the turn for a while."

Attitudes . . . especially deep-rooted ones . . . are hard to change. It can take years before the benefits emerge. Don't wait too long to begin alterations in your "new-stock attitudes." The results are usually bad if you (like the guy above) wait until a bear is chasing you to begin your aerobics program.

Bar Coding and EDI . . . Will You Need Them?

14

Sounds like a dumb question, doesn't it? *"Of course* we'll need them, Graham! Every trade journal issue in my industry these days has an article talking about one or the other . . . the great labor-savings, the sales-potential, the improvement in corporate quality." Well . . . I won't argue. I agree. Both Bar Coding and EDI (Electronic Data Interchange) seem certain to play major roles for the distributor in the years ahead. For some companies, one or both are important already.

As with any new concept, however, the early stages often involve some expensive trial and error episodes. Executives who pride themselves being in on "the cutting edge" of new technology wind up with their companies on the "bleeding edge." Oh yes . . . they eventually work out all the bugs and develop a productive system. It's just a very expensive process because they rushed into the battle without first doing some reconnaissance. The final cost of the functioning system is twice what it would have been had the boss been a bit more patient . . . waited a while for the technology to settle down, waited for the equipment costs to float down to earth, and not insisted on being the "first guy in the neighborhood" to get involved.

Remember the First Electronic Calculators?

I'm old enough to remember the old electro-mechanical calculators that cost $800 and made so much racket (if several were in a
room) that you needed ear plugs. Then dawned that wonderful day
when the first desk-top model appeared in the office that used
microchips or whatever. It cost $150, perhaps, but it did every-
thing the old models could . . . quieter, faster, and for a whole
lot less money. Today, the same functions are done by a small,
solar-powered, hand-held calculator that's so cheap it's a
throwaway when it stops working. You receive one at Christmas
from your service station with a fillup.

Should a Distributor Wait That Long to Get into Bar Coding?

No . . . I'm not advising that kind of delay. I am suggesting a
cautious approach with plenty of homework, substantial "surface-
preparation" (remember the last time you painted your house), and
as much free education from others already involved as they'll give
you. And this chapter is by no means an indepth look at either Bar
Coding or EDI. I'll just "skim through" the two subjects briefly,
offering a few important highlights and then some counsel.

Some of the material came from a two-part article on Bar Coding
by Mr. Bob Clifton that appeared some time back in "Modern Distribution Management," published by Van Ness Philip in Claverack,
NY. With apologies to Mr. Clifton, I've lifted only portions of his
complete discussion, adapted it to my writing style, and added
points here and there to help your understanding. Should you want a
more complete treatment of the topic, write or call Bob Clifton,
1149 Lafayette Road, Wayne, PA 19087. (215) 688-2748. The
opinions about the status of Bar Coding and EDI, and any counsel
regarding them, are my own . . . not Mr. Clifton's. Don't jump
him if you disagree. I'm the culprit.

UNDERSTANDING FUNDAMENTAL TERMS AND PHRASES

Bear with me now, you old timers. I realize that you already know
much of this first stuff . . . but remember that some people who

read this book will be brand new to distribution. A few right out of school. A review of fundamentals is important and it won't hurt you. Terms and phrases need definitions if we're all to speak the same language, so any discussion of Bar Coding begins with brief explanations of terms.

What's a "Code"?

A code is a set of letters, numbers, or a combination of these . . . together with spaces between groups . . . that represent information. Especially since computers came of age, codes have replaced text for brevity, clarity, computer efficiency, secrecy, and to permit the information to be shown in bar symbol form. We're all familiar with zip codes, area codes, and coding at the bottom of our checks which identify the bank and our account. I even recall a Captain Midnight secret "codagraph" ring I sent for after listening to a radio program when I was a boy (and now you know how long ago that was).

A History Lesson

I can even remember the day of the "kardex," when our posting clerks worked with item descriptions instead of part numbers or codes. Then the computer age dawned. Like everyone else, we had to develop shorter "codes" to replace those long-winded item descriptions if we were to access the computer's files quickly and efficiently. Then facsimile (FAX) transmissions became popular, and these codes offered another benefit. The shortened identifications tied up a telephone line for less time. The cost is less . . . so nearly all product part numbers these days are identified by codes of a numeric or alpha-numeric type.

Why Is This So Important?

Well, besides the obvious quality improvement within a distributor's operation, Electronic Data Interchange and many other communication forms are making rapid advances in business today. With EDI and a network interchange, incompatible computers in two different companies can talk to each other . . . making inquiries, sending orders, returning acknowledgements, forwarding invoices . . . an almost endless range of business-to-business communication. Codes provide a short, efficient way to identify company names, document numbers, part numbers and quantities and whatever else the communicators need to send back and forth. Bar coding symbology now takes the process one step farther. Bar codes convert the lengthy, detailed English descriptions of years past into a form that may be read accurately, is less costly to transmit, and isn't prone to the computer-entry-error we all suffered when human fingers were involved . . . but there's more.

Significant vs. Non-Significant Codes

A significant code is one where each digit has a specific meaning, and someone who knows the codes can "read" or interpret the

What do you mean you ordered 7613457 of them?
That's the phone number.

information conveyed. Take fasteners, for example. An item's code beginning with "S" could mean that the item is made of steel; "B" could mean brass; "A" denote aluminum, etc. The next digit might specify thread diameter. Each digit thereafter spells out another feature of the fastener. If you know what each digit specifies, and you understand the codes, then you can quickly tell precisely which fastener a particular coded number describes . . . in a manner similar to your old chemistry professor who identified $H2O$ as water.

Problems Always Crop Up

Distributors like codes like this, but there are serious limitations when a significant-code numbering system is applied in some industries. Often, far too many digits are required to fully describe all the characteristics of a product. The codes are cumbersome, hard to learn, and mistakes are common. With fasteners, the Industrial Fasteners Institute had to come up with a 31-digit number to properly cover all the features that could distinguish one item from another. A very detailed manual was required to explain the numbering system, and when new products came along, the system broke down. The coding approach just wasn't workable.

A non-significant code attacks the identification problem from another angle. A limited-length code of alpha-numeric or just numeric digits is assigned to each product, but you can't identify an item by the code itself. An "interface" or reference file is necessary . . . tied to a directory of number assignments to items . . . and some form of lookup is needed for identification. Telephone, social security, and credit card numbers are examples of the non-significant code. Your alpha-numeric auto license tag number (unless your's reads "ROAD HOG" or "BLONDIE") doesn't say anything about you. A lookup is necessary when the officer pulls you over.

Variable vs. Fixed-Length Codes

Some codes are "fixed-length," meaning that only a specified number of letters and/or numbers are permitted. Again, your Social Security number illustrates this type. Other codes are "variable-length," permitting any combination of letters and numbers up to a very generous limit, but all codes under this approach are not of the same length. Your own name illustrates a variable-length alpha code that identifies *you*. Peoples' names vary in length from very short to very long. Bar coding systems handle either type: Fixed-length or variable-length. The Universal Product Code (UPC) is fixed at 11 digits plus a check digit. Other systems allow variable length codes. However, if a code becomes too long, it may exceed the space allotted to a bar code label.

Numeric vs. Alpha-Numeric

Numbers versus letters. Although bar codes handle this problem easily, there's been confusion for many years between the letter "l" and the number "1" when seen in print or displayed on a screen. The letter "O" and number "0" are sure hard to tell apart. B's can look like 8's, and when you say one of these audibly . . . you really have trouble: "A" sounds like "8," "B" sounds like a number of others like "C," "D," "E," "G," "P," and "T." "Three" can sound like any of these as well. The military and aviation industry use "Alpha," Bravo," "Charlie," "Tango," etc., to identify letters as letters and avoid confusion between them when spoken. They'll say "niner" instead of "nine" to avoid confusion with "five," two numbers that sound alike when slurred a bit.

Common vs. Individual Code Assignment

Ah . . . common numbering for identical items, regardless of manufacturer . . . wouldn't *that* be nice? Yes it would, but you'll not likely live long enough to see that concept applied universally. Although the features which distinguish one manufacturer's products from his competitor's are often microscopic, they sure don't want their products reduced to the "commodity" category. They fight like enraged anteaters to avoid any common numbering scheme for their stuff and the other guy's. There are a few true commodities . . . black iron pipe fittings, common nails, copper wire, etc. . . . but common numbering for most other products will be resisted.

Even where there are commodities, some form of central agency is needed to assign the item codes, publish the catalogs, and promote the common code numbers to the distributors who could use them. Most of you know of industries and companies where some effort along these lines failed when there wasn't wide-spread acceptance.

ON TO THE BAR CODES

Enough about coding types and systems. Most of you knew all this already. Now let's talk about how bar codes work. A bar code is a machine-readable symbol that represents a human-readable code. Some bar code systems (or "symbologies" . . . each new technology adds its own words to our language) can represent any combination of letters and numbers. Other systems handle numeric characters only. Obviously, the proper "reader" is required to be able to interpret the bar code's meaning. Bar code readers use light beams to read a symbol of variable-width bars and spaces. It converts the information into a form the computer can use.

You probably remember the first time a supermarket checker used a bar code reader to total up your bill. I was absolutely amazed. It was faster, much more accurate, and later they added technology whereby a sweet female voice lovingly told me the prices (with the same emotion of the Atlanta airport-train voice). The Universal Product Code (UPC) had been put to very good use. Bar coding technology was the breakthrough.

Sifting All the Codes Down to a Final Few

Over 50 bar coding systems have been developed in the United States alone, with new ones still being announced. Most of these were born because some company wanting to gain a foothold in this blossoming new technology tied a unique code to their own equipment and software required to prepare or read the codes. As all this sifted down, there were exaggerated claims as to one code's superiority over another, but the problem was . . . most readers could handle only two or three codes. If you had equipment that could read codes A, B and C . . . but the supplier marked his product with code X, you were back to square 1. You had to apply your own labels to the product to use your bar coding capabilities.

An Early Attempt to Standardize

A Distribution Symbology Study Group was formed from a broad group of bar coding experts to study all the various systems and then recommend the one(s) that would serve best. These systems won out:

- Interleaved 2 of 5 — For straight numeric codes
- Code 3 of 9 (39) — for alpha-numeric codes

Interleaved 2 of 5 allows you to scan from either end. It uses an even number of numeric characters, wide or narrow bars and spaces, and density can be from 2.3 to 17.8 characters per inch depending on the printing method. Code 39 handles alpha-numeric characters of variable length and is also scannable from either end (bi-directional). Print density may be from 3 characters per inch to 9.4.

There are of course others still in use, like the Uniform Code Council's UPC used in the supermarkets; Code 128, which reduces the amount of space needed and allows special characters; and Codabar. Just as in the early days of Beta versus VHS models of video recorders, it's hard to say right now which of these codes above will eventually dominate. Perhaps we'll all learn to live with several coding systems if some solve special problems that can't be handled by a single concept. The reader/label printing equipment will just have to become more versatile as the years go by . . . but perhaps the new study now being supervised by the Uniform Code Council (more on that in a minute) will help in this area. Maybe the two codes above won't be the final winners after all. Another reason not to get into too big a rush today.

Application Standards

The various coding systems ask the user to adhere to definite standards as to where the label appears on a box or package. They might suggest four labels on each box . . . one on each side . . . to accommodate fixed beam scanners, the type used when a carton moves down a conveyor. If you select a particular system, it's very important to study carefully the literature from the central controlling agency, to be sure that you follow the application guidelines. Allow me to play "prophet" for a moment to say that this kind of rigidity will be eliminated in years to come. Already, customers are saying to a distributor:

> "Listen, I want you guys to put *our* bar code labels on the lower right side, front, of every package you send in here . . . no other place! In fact, if you fail to comply on this, we'll charge you .20 per unit to apply the labels ourselves."

A distributor's capability to apply labels of varying sizes, positioning, and even "systems" will have to be very flexible as the 21st century approaches.

Printing Your Own Labels

When suppliers or customers use incompatible coding systems, the distributor has to prepare labels to be applied to the products in Receiving before material goes into the warehouse . . . or in Shipping as the material moves out to the customer. Some distributors assign this job to a special PC (personal computer), located out in the warehouse and equipped with specialized software. The Industrial Distribution Association in Atlanta developed a listing of companies who supply software that prints bar code labels (of several types) on almost any popular PC brand.

Obviously, the distributor reaps a big advantage when the supplier ships material already bar coded under a system the distributor's equipment can read . . . like the UPC code. Fortunately, as the years move along, more and more suppliers are conforming to bar-coded packaging and to the UPC code.

SCANNING AND PRINTING EQUIPMENT

As with most new, mushrooming industries, the choices in bar code equipment for every task has exploded. A separate book would be needed to delve into all the variations (hand-held vs. fixed-position scanners, for example), the advantages and problems (scan rates, first-read rates, depths of field, non-reads, scanning windows, bar width reduction, etc.). Here I'll just point you to the places where you can learn about these things. Just as with the selection of a computer, the selection of bar coding equipment is driven by your special needs. You don't want to spend big money . . . and wind up with features you really didn't need or rarely use.

Where to Start Your Education Process

The Automatic Identification Manufacturers, Inc. (AIM USA) offers a roster of companies showing the type of scanning products they sell. Contact them at 634 Alpha Drive; Pittsburgh, PA 15238-2802. (412) 963-8588. Fax: (412) 963-8753. This organization sponsors a bureau known as "FACT" . . . the Federation of Automatic Coding Technologies, which is a group of companies interested in advancing bar coding knowledge. They may be reached at the same location and numbers, and can provide a wealth of basic information to help your understanding of the problems to be addressed and solved.

Industry Association Groups

Some distribution industries and/or their associations have formed groups to study bar coding for their businesses and recommend coding systems or to set some standards. The Automotive Industry Action Group (AIAG) was formed for the automobile industry. The address: 26200 Lahser Road, Suite 200; Southfield, Michigan 48034. (313) 358-3570. The Industry Bar Code Alliance (IBCA) works in a host of industries: heating/venting/air-conditioning/cooling (HVAC); plumbing/heating/cooling/ piping (PHCP); specialty tools; fasteners; paper trade; insulation; floor coverings; petroleum equipment; and others not so directly related to distribution. Contact them at: (215) 822-6880.

A Coordinated Effort Is Now Underway

Obviously, this fragmented industry-by-industry approach really isn't the right way to address the bar coding standards issue. Distributors who sell across industry lines need help, so a whole host of distributor and manufacturer groups have finally agreed to sit down together . . . for as long as it takes . . . and see what's required to get everyone conformed to the Universal Product Code (UPC) if that's possible. This massive effort is just beginning under the overall supervision of the Uniform Code Council; 8163 Old Yankee Road, Suite J; Dayton, Ohio 45459. (513) 435-3870.

Mr. Harold Juckett heads the council, but as this book goes to press, the UCC has added a new staff position (Mr. Tom Brady) to work with the "Industrial Advisory Committee." The Industrial Distribution Association (IDA), The National Association of Electrical Distributors (NAED), The Fluid Power Distributors Association (FPDA), The National Office Products Association (NOPA), the Health Industry Bar Code Conference, the manufacturers of scanning equipment (AIM), the chemical industry, and IBCA . . . with its list of participants mentioned above . . . along with the National Association of Purchasing Management (NAPM), are *ALL* meeting on a scheduled basis to work on the bar coding conformity issue.

The Final Decisions Will Erase All Bar Coding Headaches . . . Right?

When will they finish? Will all these industries agree to use the single UPC code? Hmmm . . . I wonder, and if they do, you may be in the nursing home. Still, that's not the point. *They've begun!* They'll set preliminary guidelines that will be of help. But in trying to find a standard for so many diverse products across so many industries, you can expect some compromises. Some groups (your's among them, perhaps) may ultimately reject the UPC approach and return to their own unique coding system. My point here: If you want to know what's happened to date in bar code standards . . . and you're ready to move into a program . . . then a call to Mr. Brady would be worthwhile. Or call Bob Clifton in Wayne, PA. (215) 688-2748. He'll represent the IDA at each meeting.

A Consultant Could Be a Good Investment Here

In a fast-changing environment like this bar coding business seems to be, you might do well to hire a consultant (not me . . . I know zilch) to guide you through the maze of system and equipment choices. The best known, primarily because he's been preaching bar coding for distributors as far back as 1985 or earlier, is Rick Bushnell; 24 Far View Road; Chalfont, PA 18914; (215) 822-6880. Yes, you'll spend some money. You'll get an education in the process and perhaps avoid some costly mistakes in how you move into your bar coding program. Mr. Bushnell is also the administrator of IBCA mentioned above, so his firm is particularly helpful in the industries served by IBCA.

Visit a Distributor Who's Been Through the Process

If you'd rather "do it yourself," part of your pre-system education should include visits to at least two other distributors who are now up and running in a fully bar coded environment. One day with them is worth 18 sales pitches from equipment suppliers. You'll find out what to do and what not to do. Frankly, you should offer to compensate them for the time they spend with you. Their counsel will be worth a lot. Here are two. One entered bar coding quite early: Commerce Electric Supply in Linthicum, Maryland. General Manager: Roy Beard (301) 636-2100. The second is a more recent convert: Precision Industries; Omaha, Nebraska. President: Dennis Circo (402) 593-7050.

ELECTRONIC DATA INTERCHANGE

EDI . . . another fast-moving capability that, in my opinion, still has some "settling-down" ahead before it delivers all the potential benefits that could smooth out communications between distributors and manufacturers. Don't miss my point here . . . EDI already *IS* important between distributors and their customers. A growing number of customers want to tie their computer to the distributor's for inquiries, price quotes, ordering, and expediting. On the other side . . . as the distributor works with his suppliers . . . the process will be slower to mature.

Direct Tie-In's Are Still Rare and Expensive

For EDI to really help the distributor, he needs to be able to inquire directly into the supplier's computer, check stock in any of several warehouses, get a current price, place an order, get back instant confirmation, check the status of an old order, and be invoiced directly over the same system . . . and do this with at least 80% of his purchasing. Today in most industries, the distributor can do that with only a very limited number of suppliers . . . maybe three or four . . . and even here there can be productivity problems (having to enter an order twice: Once in his own computer, a second time in the supplier's system.).

The "Mail Box" Approach

As the technology stands today, most distributors using EDI extensively with their suppliers do so under a "mail box" concept. They purchase software from one of perhaps 15 firms that offer a go-between capability. A purchase order to any one of 20 of their major suppliers is keyed only once into their own computer. The purchased software accepts the order also to be relayed onto the supplier's computer . . . but not immediately. It's held in "Mail Box" mode, so to speak, until the supplier's computer asks for the information. Invoicing from the supplier follows the same track back in reverse. Trouble is . . . the distributor has no direct access to the supplier's computer. The distributor can't check stock, get prices or expedite old orders. He can order and get invoiced. That's all.

Hey, It's Still Better Than the Old Ways

OK . . . it's not perfect. It doesn't provide the help that a direct tie-in does, but it *does* cut down on errors and it *does* speed up the ordering process compared to the old "type-it-and-mail-it" or "call-it-in" methods of the 70's and 80's. It's just not a lot better than a FAX, which also can be transmitted computer-to-supplier with the right software. That's why I think EDI between distributors and manufacturers still needs improvement.

The Multiple-Industry Problem

Even in an industry, as with industrial distributors, where a system like "REDINET" (now part of Sterling Software's "ORDERNET") . . . or where a major supplier's network, like General Electric's "GEISCO" . . . offers more direct access for a larger number of items under a single system, the old industry cross-over problem still surfaces to slow the distributor from true efficiency. If he markets in two other industries, the big single system offers limited EDI assistance, even if (as some do today) there's a message interchange service. Just as railroads work with each other's cars, the message interchange moves messages over to another industry network . . . but a direct tie-in is still a better approach.

A distributor in the 21st century needs the more-efficient, direct EDI access capability on at least 80% of his purchases . . . regardless of whether he's buying an electrical item, a plumbing product, or a hand tool. "Mail-Box" relays just won't get the job done. He'll need instant verification of stock condition, pricing, and ship-date. Virtually all communication with a supplier must be possible over his EDI system . . . just as it will have to be on the other side, between the distributor and his customer.

Don't Get in Too Big a Rush Here

I can envision some type of EDI study, just like the one now going on about bar coding, taking place in the next ten years. The day will come when the distributor will have direct access to almost anyone . . . of any size . . . from whom they purchase products. So my counsel? Be patient here a while longer, just as it might be wise to do with bar coding. Let the dust settle a bit more before spending big money on EDI networks or software. Most computers today can produce recommended stock replenishment orders that, after approval, need not be re-keyed. Software sends the order through the normal FAX system directly to the supplier. Unless he refuses to accept FAX orders, this method seems to offer the same error reduction and productivity savings as the "mailbox" EDI relay system.

SUMMARY

Bar Coding and EDI . . . two more technological advances that leave old-timers like me shaking their heads. "Gosh, if only Agnes who worked our kardex years ago and Louise who had to type all the purchase orders . . . and Frank, who worked out in the warehouse back in '63 . . . could see people using Bar Coding readers and EDI terminals, they'd do back flips in their graves (or in their nursing home beds)." Remarkable breakthroughs, no question about that!

Of course, my dad felt the same way about automobiles and radios. He never quite got over the advances in his lifetime brought about by those two technological breakthroughs in transportation and communication . . . but he didn't buy a car right off either. He waited to buy his first one until Henry Ford brought out the Model T . . . at $500. The 1905 models cost as much as $5,000.

I still get a nagging feeling that we're still in the early stages for both Bar Coding and EDI. Both need to settle down. The equipment/software/capability/costs/benefits are still an unbalanced mix. Rapid strides are taking place. Every distributor will use both breakthroughs as a regular course of doing business by the early days of the 21st century. It won't be long before most of the employees in your company won't even remember when bar coding wasn't used extensively and EDI wasn't the most efficient way to communicate . . . but as with those early cars, you might do well to wait a spell before plopping down huge sums to replace your horse. Two or three years of patience might save a bunch of cash and provide for you systems quite superior to what you see today.

GMROI and
Turn & Earn . . .
What's Their Value?

15

Gross Margin Return On (Inventory) Investment and Turn & Earn . . . two measuring devices that distributors have used for many years to help pinpoint problems and to guide corrective action. To question their value at all, for some executives, is tantamount to throwing doubt on "Mother, Home and The Flag." But as you know . . . figures can mislead if the conclusions are based on bad data or an incomplete picture. Since inventory is such a large percent of most distributors' assets, it follows that any standard of performance and operating measurements against the standard must be accurate and based on correct logic. That's true especially with GMROI and T & E.

GMROI

First of all, remember that Gross Margin Return on Investment is valid only when applied at the "lump" level . . . groups of items, product lines, supplier brands, total branch stock, etc. If you take it down to item level, you may get misleading feedback. Here's the formula:

$$\text{GMROI} = \frac{\text{Gross margin dollars per year on sales from stock only}}{\text{Average inventory value throughout the year}}$$

Let's put some numbers in here for one of your product lines:

$$\text{GMROI} = \frac{\$500,000}{\$620,000} = .806$$

Your $620,000 inventory investment over the course of the year (which cost 30 cents per dollar to carry or $186,000) brought in gross margin dollars of only $500,000. "Hey . . . ," you say, ". . . that's not too bad. That's a pretty nice return!" No, it isn't. The $500,000 are *gross margin* dollars . . . not net profit! Those dollars had to cover all your operating costs, all your overhead, all your debt service, all your selling expenses . . . everything. You'd have done better just to pay all those with the money you put instead into inventory. It would have been cheaper.

What's a Good GMROI to Shoot for?

So what's a *good* product line? How can you tell, via GMROI, whether the inventory investment is well-placed . . . or you'd be better off had you put the money into a CD? When the GMROI answer comes out between 1.25 and 1.75, you've got a winner. Less: You aren't getting your money's worth. More: You probably aren't carrying **enough** stock at this location in these products, or you're "killing a fat hog" with profit margins. Everyone wants higher gross margins, but if you go too far, you may find a hungry competitor chopping into business that had been your's exclusively.

TURN & EARN

A different view of the same problem is offered by Turn & Earn. It's a little like measuring temperature by Fahrenheit or Centigrade. Both GMROI and T & E reveal the same basic business problems or health. First, the distributor calculates a correct turnover factor:

<u>Total Annual Cost of Goods Sold (From Stock Only)</u>
Average Inventory Value

Or, if you're a central warehouse that takes care of other branches:

<u>Total Annual Cost of Goods Sold + Transferred Out (From Stock Only)</u>
Average Inventory Value

Note: Be sure to leave out of this calculation those transactions which did not require the use of stock (direct ships, special purchases, local pickups from competitors or warehouses, etc.) If you misfigure the turn rate, then any conclusions from the T & E measurement are wrong.

The Turn & Earn Formula

Example:

Turns × Gross Margin Percent = Turn & Earn Factor

3.2   ×   .21   =   67

You should be up around 100 or higher on Turn & Earn with a product group. That equates to about 1.33 on the GMROI scale . . . both acceptable. The logic is rather obvious: If you can make only a small gross margin because of the competitive climate, then you *must* turn the inventory faster. If on the other hand, you make a killing in margin . . . you can afford a lower turn on inventory.

How Do These Help a Distributor?

With some products, these measurements guide how selling prices are established. On repair parts, for example, you know going in that turnover will be very low . . . 2.0 or worse. Repair parts by nature sell unpredictably, erratically, and yet a wide coverage is required. You therefore try to set prices such that a higher than normal gross margin is achieved. Maybe you enjoy a product line with very high margins . . . 45 to 60%. You can afford to push that even higher, perhaps, with large-volume purchases that will result in very low turns . . . numbers that would never be permitted at only a 20% GM.

Most often, however, the two measurements simply pinpoint problem children . . . product groups and lines that are not performing profitably and need serious management attention: Too much slow & dead stock; poor buying habits; eroding margins; inadequate selling effort; lines that should be discontinued; a bad manager in that location . . . headaches like these.

Don't Take Either Measurement Down to Item Level

Just as with any measurement, you'll draw the wrong conclusion if you apply it to an area it wasn't designed to measure . . . or where there are other more important factors to consider ahead of either GMROI or T & E. A batting average of .180 is lousy . . . right? Now apply that as a *major factor* to your 23-game winning pitcher who had a 1.6 ERA last season. If you measure the guy by the wrong standard, he may be put on waivers. Your future as General Manager of that outfit is predictable.

GMROI or Turn & Earn need to be kept at product grouping levels, branch levels, vendor line totals, etc. If you try to measure the performance of an individual item, you may wind up looking like that general manager above. Consider an inexpensive seal in your stock. It costs 18 cents. You sell only 30 per year, and the average gross margin percent is only 15%. Right now, you have 27 in stock. By either measurement above, this seal is a loser. You shouldn't stock it . . . or certainly nowhere near the 27 you now have.

Wait a minute. Your total investment is a whopping $ 4.86 right now. It's a class 12 item and you should (correctly) buy a full year's supply at a time . . . which you just did. The correct turnover on this seal is 1 per year. Hang Turn & Earn! Hang GMROI. It's a lot more hassle . . . a lot more expensive . . . to special-order this seal for a customer when he orders than to keep it in stock. Less than $5 in inventory saves much more than that in paperwork and administrative costs. Plus . . . you can't sell the $ 230 motor that this seal fits if you don't have one in stock if the customer also needs it.

Oh sure . . . you couldn't allow *every* item to be handled like this, but for this seal, the two measurements we've discussed are invalid. Other considerations override what they'd tell you to do. Remember to apply both GMROI and Turn & Earn only at the "lump" level.

CONCLUSION

Both measurements can be quite helpful. One or both should be calculated at least quarterly on all product lines and all branches. Be sure to have your computer exclude items that haven't been in stock for at least six months or seasonal product lines that haven't yet had a chance to go through an entire season.

The key to both isn't the measuring. The computer can do that. Whether they'll prove helpful or not depends on your management action. What exactly do you *DO* when either GMROI or Turn & Earn uncovers a product line that isn't earning its keep? When your gas gauge reads "Empty" . . . and you keep motoring right on down the freeway . . . you can't scream: "Bad Measuring!" when you coast to a stop in a remote spot. The measuring device revealed your problem. Your inattention to it, or unwillingness to be bothered, got you stranded.

Computer Features
that Enhance or
Retard Productivity   16

Some aspects of the work I do today surprise me. I'm an inventory man. Most of my working life has been devoted to wrestling with the headaches involving which items to stock, how much and when to buy . . . but in the last few years, I've been asked to evaluate numerous software packages and suggest improvements. The software outfits will even pay for such counsel. So I've broadened my scope a bit and now delve into computer system functions and features that aren't directly related to Inventory Management . . . while in the process of offering ideas on those functions which are related. I didn't set out to do this kind of work. I'm surprised that so much of my time today is spent in these "system reviews."

The Software Houses Want to Be "Endorsed"

Another surprise is that my "endorsement" of one software package over another matters to anybody. I wasn't seeking that position either . . . but as more distributors embraced the Graham concepts of Inventory Management, then more software houses made some effort (as discussed in earlier chapters) to build the principles, disciplines, restraints, and formulas into their packages. Some did it well . . . others not so well . . . another group very badly. Someone representing a package in one category or the other calls: "Graham, we programmed our system around your book. How about telling distributors about us if one asks your opinion as they select a system?"

That's too risky without first looking in-depth at what they've done . . . and the system review evolved. Usually requiring two days, the review and critique of each system is intensive. Everything is scrutinized . . . with a special focus, of course, on Inventory Management.

This Exposes Me to Many New Ideas

Since the software people ask for advice, I'm not shy in offering it . . . and before the two days are over I've usually given them 5 or 6 major areas to work on and 150 minor enhancements to consider. Often however, I learn something from them as well. They may perform a normal function better than anyone else ever has. Their Order Entry system may have a unique feature I haven't encountered before, or they may have employed a windowing technique particularly well. Maybe their application of the Graham principles . . . the way a screen looks, the format of a report, etc., shows ingenuity . . . and sometimes they've made a major breakthrough on a problem that's stymied nearly everyone else. I try to file these ideas away to help other companies.

Then There's the Other Stuff

Unfortunately, I also see system features which function poorly. Some show a lack of system planning or perhaps ignorance of what the users really do (or should do) in the step served. Some systems have features which are even dangerous . . . things that make it just too easy for a person to hurry along without adding or using the right information. This chapter offers some of the good . . . and bad . . . features to incorporate or avoid in your next software package. They're not all of equal importance. Some are critical; others just make a system more usable.

GLOBAL DEFAULTS

The first software feature where great caution is required is the global default. It's most often used to get a new system-user up and running quickly. Rather than have the distributor's employees search out and laboriously key into the files a mountain of data . . . the system just plugs values or entries on a "global" basis. This satisfies the system's need for the information, enables orders to be priced, replenishment to take place, and functions to proceed early on . . . without someone having to enter tedious detail over and over for each branch separately. Sounds sensible, but this can lead to big trouble if applied improperly.

You'd like an example? Well, think back a moment to the chapter about Replenishment Paths for all stock items. They allow solid control. They guide just how a stock item is to be handled, depending on the source of resupply. But you're a distributor with a big central warehouse and ten branches, with a total of 150,000 SKU's (stockkeeping units . . . the number of items stocked times the locations that carry them). We're talking 150,000 independent path-code entries into the computer by the time all locations are fully operational on the new software. The distributor doesn't want to do that much work. To get underway, the systems installers are told: "Just plug in two path codes: One for the warehouse buying from an outside supplier . . . and a second code for branches who get their stock from central. We'll come back later and put in the correct codes for each item."

Big trouble right from the start! In trying to sidestep the work and take the easy way onto the system, many items are assigned incorrect codes. They get fouled up immediately. Stockouts and massive overstocks occur. The new system is graded "F" by many people all around the company: "This stupid system doesn't work! We're in a mess. We can't use it. Let's dump the whole thing and revert back to our old buying/replenishment logic."

Some "Start-Up" Work Can't Be Sidestepped

When you repaint your house, preliminary work is required ahead of the actual paint-application step. Frankly, I hate this part. I refuse to do the scraping and sanding . . . sometimes even wood replacing . . . that's necessary to have the finished job turn out well. As a result, I'm a terrible painter. My work looks shoddy and hurried. I wind up hiring others to do it right.

When the contractor starts your new house, weeks of foundation work are needed and all you see is a big hole. Nothing's visible above ground. It's frustrating when you can hardly wait to move in. In both these illustrations, however, we all recognize the need for careful, tedious, patient, expensive preparation. Experience teaches that hurrying through the foundational steps is even more expensive in the long run.

Then why do distributors resist so strongly the need for solid data preparation when starting a far-more-expensive, far-more-critical-to-survival new computer system? Hey . . . if you have 150,000 SKU's, you have a mountain of work to do. Each stock item in each location needs individual attention as you set up the files from which your new system will draw usage data, lead times, costs, or direction on how the item is to be handled. There isn't any shortcut to this. Trying to "gang" in all cost data or supplier identifications just leads to trouble later on.

Beware of "Universal" Costs or Controls

The same item may have a different supplier and cost in Branch 1 than in Branch 2 . . . but I'm dismayed at the software packages which permit (even encourage) global entries here. To save time, the supplier and cost are entered just once . . . and popped into all branch records for that item. The same occurs for the "control method." EOQ's are set up for all branches, all items, all conditions. Yes, all this certainly does save time when a new system is being installed. Your home builder could have shown more visible progress by sticking the wall studs directly into the ground. No doubt you could have moved in sooner. "Foundation time" must not be shortcut.

When the supplier, cost, and control method are (or should be) different from branch to branch . . . the system backfires almost immediately. In the early stages when each employee views the system critically . . . "We'll just see if this new-fangled computer's going to work!" . . . it fails. Their confidence in the new system is damaged seriously if not destroyed. You'll be quite a while getting those employees to trust the system in the future . . . and how long does it take to replace that bad start-up information with accurate numbers or correct controls? How many stockouts or expensive overstocks will you suffer before . . . on an item-by-item, branch-by-branch basis . . . you do the work you should have done up-front?

Are You Really Serious about "Quality" in Your Operation?

The new Quality programs that are now so popular since a "cutting edge" distributor won the Malcolm Baldrige award could almost be summed up this way:

> "It's much more expensive to do it over than to do it right the first time!"

That's true of start-up information. Take your time. Make sure each stock item in each location gets the right data entered into the files. Make sure each item is controlled by the method best suited for the replenishment conditions under which new material will be brought in. You spent quite a bundle on your new computerized system. Don't cripple it by rushing through the startup phase.

LOGICAL DISPLAY OF INFORMATION

Computer software is designed and coded by computer people . . . usually. Often they look at the vast array of information captured by the system and try to think of how best to display it. They may ask potential users for ideas, but if the data is new . . . not available before . . . they receive limited help. Or the new inquiry screen takes on the look of something similar in the last package on which the computer person worked.

The resulting screens often show far too much data or the wrong set of numbers for the task at hand. A single screen is designed to

serve both Sales and Purchasing. Too much data clutters it up. Too
many facts are shown that Sales doesn't need. Purchasing people
must wade through information of no interest to find the data they
want. We'll talk later about that. Perhaps the systems designer figured: "Hmmm, there's a field on that screen. We've got to show
something there!" Here are a couple of examples of that kind
of logic.

Suppress the Display of Zero's and Unnecessary Decimals

How many sales or history inquiry screens have you seen with long
strings of zero's, intermixed with an occasional entry that means
something? Wouldn't it have been better to leave a field blank
unless it contained a valid number? That way, you'd be able to see
the true activity very clearly.

How about stock item quantities that show four decimal
places . . . item after item, screen after screen, field after field
. . . because the distributor stocks ten items somewhere that are
actually decimalized? Admittedly, the system, the screens, the
fields all must allow the space to show decimals when they apply . . . but who says they have to appear for every item? Suppress
the last four decimals: show a quantity as 234 not 234.0000, when
you never stock or sell less than one unit of that item.

Think of how much more readable each screen appears . . . how much easier to see actual values and not make a
mistake because of all those decimals. A code in each item's master inventory record says that the item is decimalized or it isn't. If
not, the system never displays or prints decimals. If it needs them,
they appear. For some reason, systems designers rarely think like
this.

BRANCH STOCK STATUS INFORMATION

Another of my pet peeves are display screens that show data I can't
use while omitting the facts necessary to guide a decision. A common example: The inquiry that shows an item's stock status in

other branches when you don't have enough on hand locally to fill the customer's order.

A customer calls: "Harry, I need 50 of item ABC 26X." Your telephone salesman checks his inquiry screen and replies: "Gosh Louise, I seem to be out of those right at the moment . . . but I think our Houston branch has 'em. They told me just the other day that they were overstocked on some of the ABC brand products. Could I ship these 50 to you from Houston if they have 'em?" The customer answers: "Sure. No problem. I don't care where they come from, and I can wait a day or two. Just don't hang any shipping charges on me!" Your salesman now asks the computer for another display: "Let's see the status of item ABC 26X in all other branches!"

The Most Common Mistake

Most software packages that handle multi-location distributors can bring up a display quickly. Using a window, the item's status in other branches appears right on the regular sales order entry screen. The salesman moves the cursor to the location with stock . . . or enters the line number . . . and bingo, the desired quantity prints on an order to be shipped from that branch direct to the customer. Well as you know, it shouldn't be that easy to take the other guy's stock. However, that's not the main point of this discussion.

Almost without exception, the display begins by showing the "On Hand" balance in each of the other branches. Not very helpful. Often, some or all of the on-hand figure has been committed to customer orders at the other branch. Invoicing hasn't occurred yet, so the on-hand number may seem adequate to fill the inquirer's needs . . . but you can bet that other branch won't turn loose of material already committed to one of their customers, especially if they've already shipped it.

Also, there's a time problem here. The computer's job is to answer a question with complete information . . . not leave the inquirer with another question, requiring another inquiry or worse, the need to make a series of phone calls. What if the customer is waiting on the line while you find out exactly what you can do? This whole process must take place quickly.

What Information Is Truly Helpful?

You should develop a screen that returns data like this:

Item: ABC 26X   Today: June 25

Branch	Surplus	Avail.	Usage Rate	Order Point	Lead Time Days	On-Order	Due In
Houston		160	216	324	30	250	7/16
Tulsa	13	49	10	14	27		
Okla City		76	90	150	34	150	7/01
St. Louis		120	100	113	21		

The salesman is searching for 50 units of ABC 26X that some other branch can spare without harm. With the data above, he identifies quickly the branch most likely to release 50 units. The old systems don't show this kind of data. They begin with the "On Hand" numbers in each location. The salesman has to call the other branch to see if they can spare anything. This inquiry begins with surplus stock, followed by the "Available To Sell" (uncommitted) stock in each location.

Surplus is always "fair game," so to speak, so the 13 units in Tulsa are his if he wants them. Surplus, if any, always appears first on the display. Remember that surplus is a quantity calculated by the computer . . . not something left to a branch manager's discretion:

$$\text{Surplus} = \frac{\text{Any amount available that exceeds the total of}}{\text{Line Point} + \text{Order Quantity}}$$

or

Any quantity over the Maximum, if the item is
under "Min/Max" controls

However, our salesman wants 50 . . . not 13 . . . and Tulsa has only 49 total. Under Graham's rules, he can't take the other 36 (49 less the 13 surplus) anyway . . . and Tulsa would be cleaned out if company policy ignores Graham and permits him to ship all 49 to the Dallas customer. The salesman also doesn't want to split up the shipments to his customer . . . have 13 show up from one place and 37 from somewhere else . . . with two freight charges perhaps.

So Who's Most Likely to Turn Loose of 50?

Well . . . not Houston. Our salesman's memory is poor. The ABC 26X isn't one of the items with surplus stock in Houston. In fact, it's one of their better items. Houston sells over 200 per month, they have about three weeks's stock uncommitted . . . and their next P.O. isn't due in for nearly 3 weeks. They'll be touch and go on this ABC 26X. They may run out before the shipment arrives, so there's no way they'll ship 50 to some other region.

St. Louis has a lot of stock, but if they shipped out 50 at this point, they'd be way down below the Order Point. They'd have to reorder from the supplier immediately. Their lead time is 21 days . . . and they'd be left with less than 21 days of stock. Too risky. They won't release 50 to some other branch.

Oklahoma City is the best choice. If they release 50, they're down to 26 units in stock . . . but their replenishment order is due in about a week. Their usage rate is about 21 per week (90 per month), so although a bit tight, they should be OK.

Productivity . . . Once Again

Remember one of the primary objectives of a computerized system: To make each employee *very* productive. To survive in the 21st century, you must make every payroll dollar return a maximized employee effort. Here's a good example. If the inside salesman must call three or four branches to find out which one will release stock, a solid 15–20 minutes or more are required. If the display directs him immediately to the best candidate . . . in five seconds . . . and further programming permits him to key the transfer (surplus) or transfer request (non-surplus), he completes the transaction zappo and is on to the next waiting customer on the phone. Good use of his time. This inside salesman is highly paid. You want every minute of his time to count.

Oh . . . I know your immediate argument to all this: "Why not just enter a transfer to *any* branch who has enough stock? After all, you've got a sale made . . . a customer waiting . . . and the other branch may not sell the material for some time." The reasons for **NOT DOING THIS** are covered in Chapter 16 of "Distribution Inventory Management For The 1990's." As with much of the stuff in this book, you need to have read the earlier one to get the background. Here I'll just say that you'd better be ready to finance huge branch inventories if you authorize unrestricted "robbing" of all the stock in a branch by another who has a sale but no stock.

REPLACE A VALUABLE SNAP-SHOT THAT THE OLD KARDEX PROVIDED

There aren't many of us left who remember the old "kardex" days. Often today, when I mention "kardex" in a training session, I see a room full of blank stares: "What do you suppose he's talking about?," whispers one young lady to her friend. Oh true . . . there are a few distributors still using manual inventory cards, but they're few and far between. The computer era has just about obsoleted the cabinet trays and old rolling tubs in which we once kept manually-posted records of stock in the warehouse.

Trouble is . . . the old kardex portrayed a wealth of information about an item in a very useful manner. You could walk over to the files, flip open a two-card record and see an enlightening "snap-shot" of what was happening with the item. Then the computer came along. The kardex went out to the mezzanine to be placed under a tarp. Unfortunately, the revealing snap-shot capability went out there with it. The computer provides several inquiry screens, but as mentioned earlier, they often try to combine the needs of several departments (Sales, Purchasing, Accounting, etc.) into just one. A buyer or manager can finally get all the information needed, but it isn't easy. He or she has to know which series of screens to ask for . . . and in what modules to look. In some instances, critical data can't be retrieved at all.

THE THREE-PART INQUIRY A BUYER REALLY NEEDS

A Buyer or Manager needs three sets of facts at odd times about a stock item as a quick reference:

1. The current group of controls, costs, and buying parameters
2. The usage history back month-by-month for at least a year
3. The "In-Out-Balance" picture going back for 60 transactions

Each should be a separate inquiry, but they should be grouped together. The buyer asks for Number 1. One key stroke moves him to Number 2. Another key stroke and he's in Number 3 . . . or he can go directly to any of the three from anywhere else in the system via Function Keys, or whatever. With these three screens, he's able to "flip open" the computer records just as he could the old kardex files. Let's look at examples.

The "Snapshot" Summary

Here's a "snapshot" look at how things stand right now on this item in the Dallas Branch. Facts are pulled from several files and all displayed here in one place. Sure, many of these numbers will change . . . some tomorrow, many at the end of the month when

Branch Inventory Controls Screen

Part No: SKF 6203-2RS   Descr: Unmounted Bearing

Avail Bal:	134	Whse Loc:	04-018	On Order:	140
Committed:	30	Cus Backorders:	0	P.O. Due:	01/14
Supplier:	SKF	Replen Path:	01	Seasonal:	No
Rev Cycle:	2 Weeks	Replac Cost:	3.56	Avg Cost:	3.50
Usage Rage:	160	Avg LT:	4 Weeks	Last 2 LT's:	5W, 3W
Order Point:	240	Safty Allow:	80	SA %:	50%
Line Point:	320	Order Qty:	140 (A)	Inv Class:	1
Date Last CC:	12/01	Date Last O/S:	7/10	Times Out YTD:	2
Frozen:	0 Months	Freeze Reason:		Std Pack:	10

control recalculations are made, but right now . . . these are the facts. The buyer gets a good summary of how popular this item is, the current stock and purchase order status, controls now in place, when it was last counted.

More data is shown with codes. For example, the order quantity is shown as 140 with an (A) beside it. Code A means that the EOQ method is being used. Code B might mean Inventory Class method; Code C indicates Quantity-Break method, etc. Note what the screen *does not* show: Sales and profit dollars so far this year, the salesman assigned to the account, LIFO cost, etc. Somebody needs the information at times . . . but don't put it on this inquiry.

Now after a look at this information summary, the Buyer asks himself a question: "Hmmm . . . how was that usage rate of 160 per month developed? I thought we sold more than that of this item." Let's show him.

This screen show the usage activity on this item in this branch, month by month, back for at least a year. In the "Actual" column,

Usage History Screen

Part No: SKF 6203-2RS   Branch: Dallas

	Actual		Override	Reason
Dec	145	MTD		
Nov	180			
Oct	197			
Sep	96			
Aug	202			
Jul	316		170	U
Jun	115			
May	201			
Apr	144			
Mar	39		150	O
Feb	190			
Jan	165			

Codes:	MTD—Month Incomplete	U—Unusual Usage O—Out of Stock P—Promotion

usage of all types are combined. If this branch acts as a central warehouse to supply the needs of other branches, then transfers out are part of the numbers shown . . . as are kit or assembly usage, and sales of course. The buyer really doesn't need a breakdown of the categories right now. He or she doesn't care. He must prepare for *all requirements* against the stock. Some other inquiry can break down the usage into three different categories if someone wants that information. Just don't do it here.

Remember the History Override Codes?

The second column shows the "Override" History if one exists for a particular month. Chapter 6 of my earlier book explains why and how a buyer inserts revised usage figures (for forecasting future rates and setting the ordering controls) when the actual numbers include unusually large, one-time sales or periods of extended stockout, or promotional activity that may not recur this year. Two months for this item, this branch, reflect overrides.

Last July, a sale of 146 units caused the total usage to be 316. The buyer overrode that . . . removed the 146 from consideration . . . by inserting 170 in the "Override" column. The computer uses the 170 in its six-month averaging method of forecasting the usage rate to expect for this item in the months ahead. The code (U) beside the 170 entry gives the reason for the buyer's override. Note that for March, the override was necessary because of a stockout lasting over two weeks. 150 was used after that for forecasting. The 39 appears for information only. In calculating the forecasted usage rate, the computer uses the actual history for each month unless an override entry is present. Above, it averaged 180, 197, 96, 202, 170, and 115. 960 total divided by 6 equals 160 per month. The 145 isn't included yet. December isn't over. Next month, December will be added, June dropped in the averaging.

Keep the Usage History Screen
Simple and Uncluttered

Don't forget who will use this inquiry screen and why they came here for information. Usage screens in many packages I see (if they offer one at all) are crowded . . . cluttered with all manner of data the buyer doesn't want right now. Every usage category is shown separately; Month-to-date and year-to-date numbers appear for this year and last; Turnover results show for each month; Maybe even gross margin dollar totals for the item in each month. Well . . . admittedly, *somebody* at *sometime* or another may want to know all these things . . . but not here. Keep these history facts simple and straightforward. This is the usage history used by the computer to set the controls as they are today. The buyer should be able, easily, to duplicate on his hand calculator a usage rate from these numbers . . . and his answer checked for agreement with the computer's last calculation.

Transaction Review Screen

Our Buyer is really an inquisitive type. He wants to know even more about this item, or he's been asked a question: "Say Jack, who's been buying the SKF 6203-2RS from us recently?" Maybe he'd like to know where those history numbers came from that the computer showed him on the Usage History Screen. Let's give him back the old "kardex" card picture that was lost when we put the manual records out in the warehouse under the tarp six years ago.

You may never have seen information displayed exactly like this . . . but if you're a Buyer, you'll realize the value quickly. Again, this screen presents a snapshot or overview of what's been happening recently. If you have the disc space, show the last 60 transactions for this item in this branch by scrolling back to additional screens. On slower-moving items, you can limit the display to the last two years' activity.

The date appears when PO's are placed, as well as the receipt dates, so that lead times are easy to see. Cycle count dates are shown along with the effect on stock. This "In-Out-Balance Available" history verifies the usage totals seen earlier. It reflects, for example, purchase order # 4304 that required "shock" merchandise to be added to the regular EOQ . . . because replenishment was triggered when stock was way below the Order Point. We discussed this back in Chapter 9.

Transaction Review Screen

Part No: SKF 6203-2RS   Branch: Dallas

Date	Type	Cust/Supplier	Qnty Out	Qnty In	Avail For Sale Balance After Transaction
12/26	Sale	ABC Indus.	30		134
12/20	Sale	Ajax Corp.	10		164
12/17	Sale	Texas Mfg.	60		174
12/17	PO Placed	SKF PO # 4425			
12/16	Sale	Ajax Corp.	25		234
12/09	Sale	Hendricks	20		259
12/02	PO Recpt	SKF # 4304		240	279
12/01	C. Count		−1		39
11/30	Transfer	Houston	100		40
11/28	Sale	ABC Indus.	70		140
11/21	Sale	Hendricks	10		210
11/13	PO Recpt	SKF # 4220		140	220
11/10	Credit	Alamo Indus.		5	80
11/03	Sale	Alamo Indus.		5	75
10/31	Sale	ABC Indus.	100		80
10/24	PO Placed	SKF PO # 4304			
10/23	Sale	Texas Mfg.	60		180
10/21	Sale	Ajax Corp.	10		240

User Productivity . . . Always in Mind!

Here again, keep this screen as uncluttered as possible. Note that sales order and transfer numbers don't show. If someone needs to know precisely the sales order number . . . or more information about this transaction . . . he moves the cursor down alongside the entry and hits one more key. The full detail now appears on another screen: Document number, customer PO number, selling price, cost, profit margin . . . whatever. Just don't put all that here. This is a summary screen. Most of the time, the Buyer couldn't care less what the actual sales order number was when coming here for the summary picture. If he or she wants to know, another inquiry behind this one provides the full picture about any transaction.

Similarly, don't show customers' account numbers here. Tell us who they are. Provide as much of their name as you have room to show. The Buyer shouldn't have to do another lookup to find out who bought the 60 on December 17th.

SUMMARY

Maybe you understand now why your people are frustrated at times as they attempt to use your computer system. Systems designers build packages that offer "universal" displays. Anything anyone might ever want to know is crowded onto a single screen . . . or information of interest to different departments at differing times is combined. Numbers appear to four decimal positions on every item, every time, every screen . . . because 1% of the time the decimals are necessary. Zero's appear in field after field, column after column, when blanks would serve just as well and make the truly significant entries stand out. Trying to locate available stock in another branch is time consuming because the information provided doesn't give the full picture. Global defaults were encouraged to speed up the installation process . . . but this caused improper use of the system when the truly correct data was slow to replace default values (or never got into the files at all).

Most of this is just common sense . . . but with some systems designers, the sensible approach isn't very common . . . or maybe it's just that they never thought of it. We all fall victim to doing things the same way it was done in the past. You probably mow your yard in the same pattern each time. You drive to work along the same route. You have your hair cut (or "done") at the same place. Systems designers also follow the familiar path. If the last system on which they worked displayed information in a particular fashion . . . the new one will also. If no one questions why a display looks as it does, the screen never changes. The ideas presented here should cause you to re-think some of the old habits as you design or select your next system . . . the one that must keep you profitable on into the 21st century.

This Is It . . .
You're on
Your Own!

17

Well, that's it. At this juncture, I plan no more books. Hopefully, I've given you about all I know . . . all the concepts . . . all the variations . . . all the disciplines and warnings . . . all the system-selection guidance of which I'm capable. I can now go live in Colorado in the Summer and Kauai in the Winter. Wishful thinking, I admit, but gosh if you and others buy enough of these books . . . who knows?

Oh, I plan to hang around for a few more years to harass distributors and software firms about doing a better job of asset management, but in a scaled-down mode . . . not as many training sessions, workshops, consulting assignments, system reviews, etc. Frankly, I'm beginning to dread airports, hotels, room service, taxis, and babies crying in the airplane seat just behind mine. This news will be welcomed by a host of software firms: "Graham can't slow down (or quit) soon enough for us. We'll be happy to reserve him a spot in the Golden Age Nursing Home *today!*"

Why? My Counsel Is too Tough for Them

These software outfits try to sell their package to distributors:

- On the merits of the Accounting features, or . . .
- To a particular industry based on many users in that arena, or . . .
- On marvelous flexibility that puts no restraint on anyone, or . . .
- On their reputation as a "leading-system" (of the past), or . . .
- By association with a well-recognized hardware supplier, or . . .
- On how the "founding-father" distributorship worked, or . . .
- All of the above.

This book had better not fall into their hands. It'll become the start of a nice campfire. "Graham's too rigid! He wants to restrict what salesmen do . . . what the buyers do . . . how Management thinks . . . when some of our users *don't want to be restricted* like that. Besides, it would cost us a fortune to make our system conform to many of these unnecessary features."

True . . . Distributors Are Hard to Change

Part of their argument is true: Distributors, as a rule, are not very open to changes in operating philosophy. Many are still Sales Dominated, just as they've been since ol' Mr. Jackson founded the place in 1948. Getting them over into the Sales "Oriented" mode is akin to changing a Redskin fan into a rabid Cowboy supporter. (Quite necessary, if you're to back the repetitive Super Bowl winner of the 21st century).

Some distributors still allow the Controller to call all the shots on the computer and its system. If a new system satisfies him or her, and the Sales Manager likes the sales reporting features . . . the software salesman knows that 95% of the time, he'll sign them up. The President delegates the whole system-selection process. He doesn't want to be bothered with all the details he'd have to learn to have an effective role in the decision.

Other companies are simply afraid of their sales force. They don't **dare** bring a new system in that restrains what a salesman or a branch manager can do. Shoot, some of 'em might quit. Management continues to allow huge inventories all over the place, to buy in the "last column" regardless of justification, and to permit all manner of sloppy practices . . . things they'd never think of doing if they ran a football team or a bank. Can you imagine a football coach who was afraid to pull a sloppy player from the game, or to call a certain play, because he didn't want to irritate the quarterback? Picture a bank president who lets anybody wander inside the vault. He's afraid to restrain a long-time employee who argues: "What's the matter? Don't you trust me?" A distributor thinking like these two wants a computerized system that goes along with his management style. No restraints. No irritation of key players. No true management of assets.

The bankruptcy court dockets are crowded today with cases involving distributors like this. Until the wolf came crashing through the door, however . . . not merely growled out there on the front porch . . . the backward-thinking distributor executive didn't change. Oh yes . . . *THEN,* he or she scrambled madly to dump the bad system, find a new one to guide/restrain/help manage inventories, and finally adopt a new management approach. It was too late. The wolf simply ate him and his company. Remember the old adage:

> "Don't wait until a bear is chasing you to begin your aerobics program!"

Many Software Firms Still Prefer the Easiest Selling Approach

So I guess I can't place too much blame on those software firms who reject my concepts and rigid disciplines in asset management. After all, they want to make some sales. If a prospect balks at restraints on his managers, salesmen or buyers . . . it's an easier sale if the software house simply agrees to provide what that distributor wants. The system is "loosey-goosey" to the point of absurdity, but the salesman has a car payment due soon on his new Porche.

My counsel to *you*, Mr. or Ms. Distributor President, is to avoid a mindset like this . . . or you'll lead your company into a trap as you select your next system. Listen to the system salesman who talks of new restraints, new disciplines, a new operating philosophy, the need for extensive training . . . and offers a computerized package designed accordingly.

THE LIST OF RECOMMENDED SYSTEMS

If you don't know where to start in your search for improved software, you may contact me. I'll send the current list of systems I now recommend. The address and telephone:

> Gordon Graham   Tele: (214) 231-2215
> 913 Loganwood Ave.   Fax: (214) 231-6536
> Richardson, TX 75080

The List Certainly Has Critics

As stated in my earlier book, if no one answers your request . . . I've likely been abducted, shot, or otherwise neutralized by one of the software outfits that isn't on the list. Boy, some of them get really irate when a prospect says that he or she will consider only the listed packages. Lately they've been answering:

> "No . . . our system isn't on Graham's list. You have to pay him to get on it. We were unwilling to do that."

What's the Process Required to Be Listed?

Only part of the statement above is true. A systems house *does* have to pay me to review their package and make recommendations for improvement. The review requires two full days. Nearly every facet of their package and company is checked out for a lack or weakness in these areas:

- File Structures and Content
- Sales Order Entry Screens and Steps

- Special Order-Type Handling
- Non-Stock Order Processing
- Windowing Capability
- Sales Order Processing
- Customer Backorder Handling
- Branch Inventory Information Access
- Data Capturing For Inventory Control
- Forecasting Methods
- Capability To Identify Exceptions
- Monthly Exception Reports
- Control-Freeze Features
- Control Calculation Methods
- Branch Replenishment Path Codes
- Branch Transfer Restraints
- Cycle Count Assistance
- Bar Coding Capabilities
- Rebate Handling
- Blanket Order/System Contract Capability
- Stock Information Screens
- Recommended Action and Expediting Reports
- Dead Stock Analysis Capability
- Quantity-Discount Evaluation
- Pre Price-Increase/Promotion Evaluation
- Item Costing Methods
- Accounting Features
- System marketing approaches
- Company financial strength and organization

The review often takes place at the Dallas facility of a major hardware supplier on which the software runs. Sometimes it's at the home office of the software firm. Either way, I ask the systems people to videotape our two days together. They record every minute of our conversations. They capture each screen critique, each question, each answer, all 20 minutes that I'm at an erasable board going over the details of branch-transfer control requirements, the counsel and advice on the best ways to market the package in certain industries . . . everything is recorded on video.

Usually, I wind up specifying three or four major areas they must address if the system is to conform to my concepts . . . functions or steps related directly to Inventory Management. 150 other suggestions may be more in the realm of "helpful in selling the package" category or cosmetic enhancements to improve the user's productivity.

What's Next?

Now here's the error in that statement above made by the non-listed system: Going through the two-day review process . . . and paying my fee as counselor . . . *does not guarantee* that the software will be approved and added to the recommended system list. The software people carry the video tapes home, along with all the notes they've taken. They must first decide if they want to make the major changes I've outlined. Often they know that the required enhancements need several months of system design and programming effort at significant expense. Not infrequently, the software executives decide that the changes would cost too much . . . or that (after exposure to Graham and his concepts first-hand) they don't want to be so tightly restrained in the inventory control features offered to their prospects. I don't argue nor get mad at them. I just don't add that system to my list.

Getting Endorsed or "Certified" . . . Whatever

If they do proceed on the changes, I look at the system again when they're finished . . . usually for only one day and at their facility. Again, they pay me a fee for this second review. If the system now conforms in the major inventory management areas; if the proper restraints have been added; if the company is dedicated to a marketing effort which emphasizes the need for user-training . . . *then* the software goes on my recommended list. If they messed up or misunderstood something important, I may wait until I'm assured that they have it right.

To remain on the list, I need a good evaluation later from users. At some reasonable point in the future, I'll must talk to a company or two using the revised version of the package . . . to see how effectively they were trained, how well the system functions, etc. I've endorsed software for a while, only to stop later if the company proves deficient in training, support, uses unethical selling practices, or doesn't actually program certain features that were promised in the design phase. The primary point of all this: Over 50 software packages have been reviewed thus far. Only some 15 are on the approved list right now. Paying the review fee *does not* guarantee that a system will be certified.

The List Serves Two Purposes

I have to admit that not every package on my current list went through all the precise steps above. The more highly-recommended companies did . . . but the list has more than one purpose. If a distributor is free from hardware restraint . . . which means you may select any software you please because you're also going to change hardware at the same time if necessary . . . the list offers the best packages on the market. These software firms have gone through all the steps above, and most run on several hardware brands and models.

If you **are** hardware-restrained . . . just bought an IBM AS400 last year, for example, and management would now have apoplexy (sudden loss of bodily function) if you proposed a change . . . then I've listed at least one acceptable package to run on that equipment. It may score only a 7 on a scale of 1 to 10, compared to the better software, but it's the best I've found for your particular hardware and operating system. Some referrals like this have not conformed their package as closely as I'd like to what was recommended when it was reviewed . . . or they continue to offer several variations to the Graham concepts and/or restraints if a prospect insists.

You have this promise: I'll continue the search for packages that do conform more closely . . . and when they're found, they'll replace these marginal systems on the approved list. My objective is develop an ever-better roster of the finest software offered to distributors, and to recommend a solid package for every hardware type. As stated in an earlier chapter, I schedule more and more system reviews each year. The list has improved in quality . . . continues to do so . . . and hopefully, will offer even better software options in a year or two.

SUMMARY

So what overall conclusions should you have drawn from this book? Hopefully, these fifteen major points:

1. Mismanaged assets continue to plague wholesale distributors. It's the No. 1 cause of bankruptcy in the 1990's and likely will lead to even more business disasters in the 21st century. If you missed *that* message, you should avoid books as an educational medium.

2. Computers offer distributors . . . but particularly the outfits with annual sales of $3 to $100 million . . . a chance to compete with the "giants" that are now emerging in most industries.

3. To survive, however, a distributor's computer system must promote a very high level of employee productivity . . . and maximum return from every inventory dollar invested. "Quality" isn't something the distributor seeks to win an award . . . it's a way of life.

4. There are systems on the market today that do a much better job in both productivity-enhancement and inventory-investment-return than those available just five years ago.

5. Trouble is . . . most distributors couldn't (or wouldn't) use such improved software. They're undisciplined, keep sloppy records, allow abominable practices in both areas above and still manage in a sales-dominated mode. They fail

to see their inventory as dollar bills sitting out on the shelves.

6. For those that want to change, the system-training required will be much more extensive. They'll must be willing to pay for this. The better software packages are more like "flying" than "driving." Installation requires more time, pain and expense.

7. These systems also require better personnel in Purchasing, Warehousing, and Branch Management. Buyers and warehouse people should be paid more ..and more professionalism required of them. Branch managers must become asset managers as well as sales administrators . . . and their compensation plans reflect it.

8. There are numerous software firms that still offer old-fashioned, stodgy, "free-as-a-bird" systems that allow any buying practice, put no restraints on anyone (particularly salesmen), and worse . . . fail even to warn an employee when they're about to make a poor financial decision. These systems still sell briskly to distributors who are naive as to what they'll need by the year 2000.

9. With the Graham concepts, there are exceptions to nearly every rule. Seasonal items must be handled differently; High-volume, big-dollar items also; Rebates, Systems Contracts, and Protected Stock offer their own unique challenges where normal rules don't fit. You and your software must handle each one correctly.

10. Branches offer another group of challenges and potential profit-pits that can suck a distributor under. Special software features and new operational disciplines are needed when you're a multi-branch company that can't afford out-sized inventories.

11. Important considerations should be addressed *first* before your company opts for central or regional warehouses.

12. There are a few tricks if your company is in crisis-mode and dollars must be pulled back out of inventory . . . but these are always to be employed sparingly and on a short-term basis. They must *not* become a way of life.

13. Adding new items in the years ahead should be done under a mind-set different from that of the 1980's. Not every Tom, Dick, Harry and Jane should be allowed to add new stock items. Commitments are vital.

14. Bar Coding and EDI are coming on strong . . . everyone will need and use them before long. A little patience right now, however, to wait for both to settle down could save significant money and retraced steps by the end of the 90's.

15. Telephone technology, as well as simple changes in the way a computer displays information, can significantly enhance

the salesman's productivity . . . or the buyer's. Every pay-roll dollar must pay back maximum dividends by 2000, so these capabilities must be found out there on the market and included in the distributor's new system.

As the old sergeant used to say on "Hill Street Blues" when the teams left each day for the city streets:

"It's a jungle out there. Be careful . . . and good luck!"

Index